NEW DIRECTIONS FOR HIGHER EDUCATION

Martin Kramer
EDITOR-IN-CHIEF

The Campus-Level Impact of Assessment: Progress, Problems, and Possibilities

Peter J. Gray
Syracuse University

Trudy W. Banta
Indiana University–Purdue University Indianapolis

EDITORS

Number 100, Winter 1997

JOSSEY-BASS PUBLISHERS
San Francisco

378.199
C 453

THE CAMPUS-LEVEL IMPACT OF ASSESSMENT:
PROGRESS, PROBLEMS, AND POSSIBILITIES
Peter J. Gray, Trudy W. Banta (eds.)
New Directions for Higher Education, no. 100
Volume XXV, Number 4
Martin Kramer, Editor-in-Chief

Microfilm copies of issues and articles are available in 16mm and 35mm, as well as microfiche in 105mm, through University Microfilms Inc., 300 North Zeeb Road, Ann Arbor, Michigan 48106-1346.

ISSN 0271-0560   ISBN 0-7879-9824-9

NEW DIRECTIONS FOR HIGHER EDUCATION is part of The Jossey-Bass Higher and Adult Education Series and is published quarterly by Jossey-Bass Inc., Publishers, 350 Sansome Street, San Francisco, California 94104-1342. Periodicals postage paid at San Francisco, California, and at additional mailing offices. POSTMASTER: Send address changes to New Directions for Higher Education, Jossey-Bass Inc., Publishers, 350 Sansome Street, San Francisco, California 94104-1342.

SUBSCRIPTIONS cost $54.00 for individuals and $90.00 for institutions, agencies, and libraries.

EDITORIAL CORRESPONDENCE should be sent to the Editor-in-Chief, Martin Kramer, 2807 Shasta Road, Berkeley, California 94708-2011.

Cover photograph and random dot by Richard Blair/Color & Light © 1990.

Jossey-Bass Web address: http://www.josseybass.com

Printed in the United States of America on acid-free recycled paper containing 100 percent recovered waste paper, of which at least 20 percent is postconsumer waste.

CONTENTS

EDITORS' NOTES

Background

As the assessment movement reaches the end of two decades of intense activity, it is natural to ask the question: Has it made a difference? Even more important than a simple yes or no answer are the lessons learned from the successes and failures that the movement has had over the last fifteen years in trying to make a difference in the lives of students and in the culture of higher education institutions.

In the book *Making a Difference: Outcomes of a Decade of Assessment in Higher Education* (1993), Trudy W. Banta and Associates provided important insights based on first-person accounts by people who had developed and implemented campus assessment practices. *Making a Difference* is a useful compendium of lessons learned and examples of cases in which assessment made a difference during the first decade of the movement.

However, the question remains: Has all of the activity made a difference? For example, in an invited presentation at a conference on the National Assessment of Public School Students' Learning, Joe M. Steele (1996, p. 2) drew the following conclusions, based on survey and focus group research, in addition to American College Test's (ACT) experience in serving the needs of postsecondary institutions over the past twenty years: "First, despite exemplary efforts in outcomes assessment, results for the majority of assessment programs have been disappointing. Colleges and faculty lack consensus on what should be measured and how it should be measured. Neither colleges nor external agencies appear aware of the necessity to provide structures and funding to reward and sustain change efforts.

"Second, many past efforts at assessing and improving programs have provided little evidence of effectiveness in developing general skills essential for college graduates. There is even less evidence that colleges use assessment results for planning."

In addition, Thomas Angelo (1996, p. 3) notes that "everywhere we look, more people in more institutions are doing more assessment than ever before." However, he asks, "After more than a decade of assessment practice, where are

1

the expected gains in student learning? The evidence of improved perfor-mance, effectiveness, or efficiency? The breakthroughs in productivity? Why hasn't all this well-intentioned assessment activity led to more valuable, visi-ble learning outcomes?"

The purpose of this sourcebook is to help answer these questions. *The Campus-Level Impact of Assessment: Progress, Problems, and Possibilities* aug-ments previous accounts by presenting longitudinal case studies of selected institutions that document both progress and problems encountered thus far in the second decade of the assessment movement. These case studies and the other chapters in the volume examine why assessment has or has not made a difference.

Framework

Since 1989, Peter J. Gray's Campus Profiles column has appeared in the bimonthly periodical *Assessment Update,* which is edited by Trudy W. Banta. This column focuses on all kinds of institutions that have made serious attempts to design and implement assessment programs. Approximately twenty institutions have been profiled since 1989. This sourcebook features case studies of five of the campuses that were profiled before 1994. In addi-tion, there is an initial chapter, which provides an overview of the literature on leadership and the change process as it applies to an innovation like assess-ment. There is also a concluding chapter in which the other chapters are dis-cussed in light of ten principles of good assessment practice.

In Chapter One, Gray defines assessment as an innovation and notes that the adoption of an innovation is a process and not an event. This process is facilitated by strong and consistent leadership and a clear understanding of the change process. By providing an overview of the literature on leadership and the change process, the chapter provides a conceptual framework for assess-ing the factors that influence progress and problems, as represented in the case study chapters.

Chapters Two through Six present case studies of institutions where stu-dent outcomes assessment has existed for many years. Chapter Two by Jack Magruder, Michael A. McManis, and Candace C. Young describes the history of assessment at Truman State University (formerly Northeast Missouri State), which began in the early 1970s. They look at the early stimulus for change, identify the factors that facilitated progress over all those years, and consider the problems that have blocked progress. Chapter Three by Catherine A. Palomba contains an overview of Ball State University's academic assessment program. It traces the beginnings of the program, reviews its present state, and looks into the future. Several of the core assessment activities are described as are the areas of strength in the assessment program and the challenges to con-ducting successful assessment. Chapter Four by A. Michael Williford describes an institutional commitment to assess students at Ohio University, which began in 1981 and has grown steadily. Today, it is a commitment to continual student assessment. In this chapter, two phases of the Ohio University assessment experience are described—university-wide assessment and department-based assessment. Also discussed is the future direction for assessment at Ohio University, including potential obstacles and the need for flexibility in responding to change. Chapter Five by James R. Hurtgen analyzes the history of assessment at the State University of New York College at Fredonia. A special element of that history was the effort to revise the general college program. After a thorough review of the program was conducted, a decision was made to assess whether it was meeting its professed learning goals. The evaluation process was guided by a system of assessment-based planning and a university-wide assessment initiative that had been instituted. This chapter concludes with reflections on subsequent signs of progress and problems, which will influence the future of assessment at Fredonia. In Chapter Six, the last case study chapter, R. Dan Walleri and Juliette M. Stoering look back to the late 1970s and the budget constraints and accountability concerns that led to the reassessment of Mt. Hood Community College's mission. From that point of view, they follow the story of assessment from its origins in the emphasis on at-risk students in vocational programs to its current emphasis on institutional effectiveness. They provide a very candid assessment of what worked and what did not work at Mt. Hood, as well as some important insights about the factors that can facilitate effective assessment and institutional change.

In the final chapter, Banta discusses the enabling conditions and the stumbling blocks to moving assessment forward. In order to do so, she draws materials from the other chapters to illustrate ten principles of good assessment practice.

References

Angelo, T. A. "Transforming Assessment: High Standards for Higher Learning." *AAHE Bulletin,* 1996, *48* (8), 3.

Banta, T. W., and Associates. *Making a Difference: Outcomes of a Decade of Assessment in Higher Education.* San Francisco: Jossey-Bass, 1993.

Steele, J. M. "Postsecondary Assessment Needs: Implications for State Policy." *Assessment Update,* 1996, *8* (2), 2.

Peter J. Gray
Trudy W. Banta
Editors

PETER J. GRAY is associate director, Center for Instructional Development, Syracuse University.

TRUDY W. BANTA is vice chancellor for planning and institutional improvement, Indiana University–Purdue University Indianapolis.

By viewing assessment as an innovation to be adopted by the people in a particular institutional setting, it is possible to identify those aspects of leadership and planned change that will most facilitate its successful adoption.

Viewing Assessment as an Innovation: Leadership and the Change Process

Peter J. Gray

Like many other educational innovations, assessment was founded on great expectations. These included expectations for more efficient educational programs and expectations for more effective student learning. Of course, these expectations imply that educational institutions and their programs were not already efficient or effective enough. Whether or not these assumptions are true in general for higher education or in particular for individual institutions and their programs, there has been relentless pressure for assessment (and the expectations associated with it) over the last ten to fifteen years. And, many authors have complained that the assessment movement has not transformed higher education into a paradigm of efficiency and effectiveness even after such a long period of time.

Unfortunately, such criticism seems to be based on another assumption; that is, that higher education is some sort of monolith (like a giant corporation) that can be subjected to a singular idea, such as Total Quality Management, and, as a result, produce better student learning in a more efficient and cost-effective manner. Not only do institutions of higher education have a great deal of autonomy but also the units within the institutions and the faculty who work within the units are largely independent, all of which militates against the monolithic implementation of any innovation.

Instead of starting with the assumption that educational institutions and their programs are not efficient or effective enough, one would do better to begin with an assumption that is both more realistic and more positive: all organizations and individuals need to change and grow in order to adapt to current conditions. Faculty in particular are by education and by their very nature professionals who are curious and intrinsically motivated to question.

These characteristics form a natural propensity for such professionals to embrace the purpose of assessment, which is to bring about continual improvement. Emphasizing the role of assessment in bringing about continual improvement can help faculty members understand that engaging in assessment can be in their own self-interest, because it can give them information that will allow them to attract and retain students. In addition, by keying into their inclination to question, it is possible to provide a rationale for faculty use of assessment that reduces the level of threat and acknowledges and builds on all the good work that people have done in the past.

Recognizing that it is individual faculty members who must adopt assessment as an innovation suggests that the unit of analysis for the success of an assessment program should not be the whole of higher education, a state higher education system, or even an entire institution. Instead, the unit of analysis for determining the success of an assessment program should be the faculty within a unit (for example, a department, program, school, or college). And the criterion for success should be their commitment to continuous improvement. This focus brings us to a consideration of how change occurs.

Innovation

To understand what factors either inhibit or facilitate the adoption of an innovation like assessment it is useful to look at the literature on innovation. As defined by Rogers (1995, p. 11), "An innovation is an idea, practice, or object perceived as new by an individual." He goes on to say that "it matters little, as far as human behavior is concerned, whether or not an idea, object, or practice is 'objectively' new in the sense of the time lapse since its first use or discovery. It is the perceived newness of the idea for the individual that determines his reaction to it. If the idea seems new to the individual, it is an innovation."

As much as the idea of assessment has been discussed in publications and conferences such as those sponsored by the American Association for Higher Education, many faculty only become aware of its existence when it is introduced on their campus or in their own department.

The assessment process is complex and individuals are unique. Therefore, there are several variables that "influence the adoption or rejection of new ideas: the situation; the personality; the social and economic status of the adopter; the lines of communication used; and the innovation itself" (Rogers 1968, p. 68). This information argues for the particularization or local adaptation of assessment, as these variables are idiosyncratic to each institution, department or program of study, and faculty member.

There are several other characteristics that seem to affect the rate at which innovations are adopted (Rogers, 1995, pp. 15–16):

> *Relative advantage* is the degree to which an innovation is perceived as better than the idea it supersedes. . . .

Compatibility is the degree to which an innovation is perceived as being consistent with the existing values, past experiences, and needs of potential adopters. . . .

Complexity is the degree to which an innovation is perceived as difficult to understand and use. . . .

Trialability is the degree to which an innovation may be experimented with on a limited basis. . . .

Observability is the degree to which the results of an innovation are visible to others.

Rogers observes that educational innovations are often perceived as having little relative advantage over existing ideas, as having low compatibility with current values and past experiences, and as having low visibility of their results (1968, p. 68).

Assessment has many of these disadvantages. It can be perceived to have low relative advantage over current practices that faculty use to provide themselves with feedback on the effectiveness of their instruction in promoting student learning. It can be perceived to have low compatibility with existing values (such as academic freedom). This may be especially true for those faculty not accustomed to professional accreditation, for which assessment is related to external accountability. Unless it can be divided into manageable stages and tried on a limited basis in a way that is adapted to local conditions, assessment can be perceived as a monolithic and inflexible innovation. Because of all its jargon, complex procedures, and technical aspects, assessment can be perceived as difficult to understand and difficult to use. The results of assessment may take years to be revealed. And they may be observable only to individuals in relation to their own courses and programs. Therefore, assessment can be viewed as being low in observability from an institutional perspective and even more so from a state or national perspective.

In order to overcome these disadvantages, the introduction of assessment should be a process of planned change. There are two critical aspects of such a process—leadership and a well-thought-out series of activities that move assessment from innovation to institutionalization.

Leadership

Assessment must be made a priority over an extended period of time by central and local leaders. "Leaders . . . are those persons or groups who can mobilize human, material, and symbolic resources toward specific ends. . . . Mobilizing resources in any social system depends upon the ability of leaders to direct the behavior of others" (D. M. Rosen, cited in Curry, 1992, p. 20).

As Palmer (1993, p. 9) suggests, "The most powerful kind of leadership is to offer people pathways and permissions to do things they want to do but feel unable to do for themselves. That sort of energy evokes energies within people that far exceed the powers of coercion." Such leadership taps into people's intrinsic motivation for competence, success, quality, and continual improvement.

It has been noted that leadership in colleges and universities has some unique demands, as these are professional organizations, "where [individuals] can act as if [they] are self-employed yet regularly receive a paycheck. [They are seemingly] upside-down organization[s], where the workers sometimes appear to manage their bosses" (H. Mintzberg, cited in Curry, 1992, p. 21).

Curry (1992) explains that, consistent with the culture of a professional organization, "Members of the academy do not expect changes to come as dicta from inaccessible individuals" (p. 22). In other words, "When members of an organization enjoy a fair amount of autonomy, such as enjoyed by faculty, decisions related to implementing and institutionalizing innovations cannot be made unilaterally and be expected to go uncontested" (p. 22). As a result, academic leaders must be aware that, "Although it is possible to gain compliance or participation in the change process within professional organizations, it is not possible to legislate commitment and the support needed to institutionalize an innovation" (p. 23).

There are four management competencies that organizational leaders must have if they are to gain faculty commitment to and support of assessment: the management of attention, through a set of intentions or a vision, in the sense of outcomes or direction; the management of meaning, through the communication of this vision; the management of trust, through reliability and constancy; and the management of self—through the capacity to know one's own skills and to deploy them effectively (W. Bennis, cited in Curry, 1992, p. 20). Leaders in academic institutions who possess these competencies can reinforce both the questioning nature of the faculty and their intrinsic motivation to bring about continual improvement. In this way, leaders can encourage practice and experimentation with assessment, which will help overcome some of the disadvantages discussed earlier. However, faculty must perceive that the innovation—assessment in this case—is "necessary, beneficial, or, at the very least not harmful to the organization or to what they perceive as their domain and interest" (Curry, 1992, p. 23), which means that faculty must believe that assessment has a relative advantage over current activity.

Curry (1992, pp. 23–25), citing many different authors, has identified several roles that organizational leaders can play to facilitate change:[1]

> Organizational leaders play an important role in preparing the organization for change and for its institutionalization by creating a climate in which change can take place or by influencing the perceptions and attitudes of the organization's members. When an organization's leaders develop that climate, they in effect are beginning the process of change.
>
> [Organizational] leaders help to define and shape issues giving rise to innovations, identifying the organization as an environment where innovation and change can take place, facilitating discussion among the organization's mem-

bers, and promoting fuller participation in innovative activities. They bring
participating members into the decision-making process. . . .

[Organizational] leaders help to build community-wide coalitions in support of
change and monitor many of the key processes.

[Organizational leaders can provide] funding and other incentives for participation in the process of change. . . .

[Organizational] leaders are sponsors of change, working toward the synergy
that develops when the power of such leadership is shared, that is, the power
to propel the community forward to bring about change. . . .

[Organizational leaders perform such facilitative tasks] as gathering information,
communicating with other members of the organization, developing new
coalitions, and identifying existing coalitions that perceive their members as
stake holders in the process. . . .

[Organizational] leaders must be visionary in initiating change[, but] communications and decision making in professional organizations must be two
directional or the culture emerging from the change will not be shared.

Another type of leader is the opinion leader, who can influence others'
attitudes and behaviors in relation to a particular innovation. These leaders are
part of the social system, and they earn and maintain their positions through
"technical competence, social accessibility, and conformity to the system's
norms" (Rogers, 1995, p. 27). Organizational leaders must work to convince
these informal opinion leaders of the desirability of an innovation like assessment in order to enlist their support for change. To provide the type of leadership just described and to enlist the support of local opinion leaders,
organizational leaders must think about the adoption of innovation as a change
process.

Change Process

Many times, the introduction of an innovation like assessment is seen as an
institutional event, and the assumption is made that adoption will be accomplished just because a decision maker has announced it. However, as Hall,
Loucks, Rutherford, and Newlove (1975, p. 52) have pointed out, "Innovation
adoption is a process not a decision-point—a process that each innovation user
experiences individually." Therefore, they define change as a process not an
event, which is undergone by individuals first, and then institutions. The
change process is a highly personal experience that entails developmental
growth in feelings, skills, and knowledge.

Two hierarchies have been created for analyzing the state of growth of the
potential adopter of an innovation. One focuses on the individual's stage of
concern regarding the innovation (Hall, Wallace, and Dossett, 1973), and the
other focuses on the individual's use of the innovation (Hall, Loucks, Rutherford, and Newlove, 1975).

The stages of concern plot the developmental phases that the individual goes through in adopting an innovation. The stages of concern begin at the point of awareness of an innovation. There may be many people in an organization who simply are not aware of an innovation when it is first introduced and for some time afterward. Once people become aware of an innovation, they may progress to the stages of gathering information about the innovation and determining the personal impact of adopting it. These stages may be followed by a stage concerned with how best to manage the process and tasks of the innovation. Only after the innovation has become routinized in this way does an individual become concerned with its impact. In the case of assessment, improved student learning is often the impact intended. When an adopter is satisfied with the impact, concern may move to the stage of collaboration and cooperation with others around the innovation. It is at this point that a department-wide assessment program may be adopted. The last stage of concern focuses on how to improve the innovation or find an even better alternative. The drive for continual improvement can motivate an individual or group to move through the stages again in pursuit of an even more effective innovation.

Based on materials developed by the Research and Development Center for Teacher Education, University of Texas at Austin, for a concerns-based consulting-skills workshop, and described in Hall, Wallace, and Dossett (1973), and Hall, George, and Rutherford (1979), the stages of concern are:

Awareness: I do not know or am not concerned about the innovation.
Informational: I would like to know more about the innovation.
Personal: I want to know how using the innovation will affect me.
Management: I am focusing on the processes and tasks of using the innovation in a more or less rote manner.
Consequence: I am focusing on the impact of the innovation.
Collaboration: I am focusing on coordination and cooperation with others regarding the use of the innovation.
Refocusing: I am turning my attention to improving the innovation or seeking something that might work even better.

Levels of use "are distinct states that represent observably different types of behavior and patterns of innovation use as exhibited by individuals and groups" (Hall, Loucks, Rutherford, and Newlove, 1975, p. 54). These are parallel to the stages of concern and begin with nonuse, in which no action is taken because the individual is not aware of the innovation. Once awareness is achieved, an orientation process is begun as information about the innovation is sought. An individual then moves to a level of use in which activity focuses on becoming prepared to use the innovation, which in turn leads to the rather rote or mechanical day-to-day use of the innovation. This level of use is akin to the routinization mentioned in relation to the stages of concern and, eventually, through this process, the use of the innovation becomes stable, and refinements can be made to enhance its use. Having become comfortable with the use of the innovation, individuals can begin to integrate their own uses with the uses of others. Finally, a user or group of users will begin to assess the innovation itself and, if appropriate, to modify or replace it.

Based on materials developed by the Research and Development Center for Teacher Education, University of Texas at Austin, for a concerns-based consulting-skills workshop, and described in Hall, Loucks, Rutherford, and Newlove (1975), the levels of use are:

Nonuse: The potential user is taking no action with respect to the innovation.
Orientation: The user is seeking information about the innovation.
Preparation: The user is preparing for first use of the innovation.
Mechanical use: The user is focusing on the short-term, day-to-day use of the innovation with little time for reflection.
Routine and refinement: The user is becoming more comfortable with the innovation, so use is stabilizing, and the user is varying the implementation of the innovation to increase its impact on clients in that user's sphere of influence.
Integration: The user is making a deliberate effort to coordinate with others in using the innovation.
Renewal: The user is reevaluating the quality of the use of the innovation and seeking major modifications or alternatives.

Working people through these stages of concern and levels of use takes careful planning. This is not necessarily a linear process, but rather a recursive one, and people may be at different levels or stages in relation to different elements of an innovation. And, of course, it is likely that different people in a unit will be at different levels and stages in relation to a given innovation. Therefore, support for innovation adoption needs to be extended across several cycles of use and over an extended period of time, rather than focusing on a single experience or short-term series of events.

To understand better this differentiation of users—which refers to the user's receptivity toward an innovation and the speed at which an innovation is adopted—one can learn from Rogers (1995), who identified five types of users of innovations distributed over a normal distribution of a population. These five types can be described as follows:

Innovators, those first few people in a group to use an innovation. These are the experimenters, who make up the first 2.5 percent of the population.
Early adopters, those for whom the innovation may be easily adopted. These are the visionaries and risk takers, who do not fear failure. They make up the next 13.5 percent of the population.
Early majority, those who may be comfortable with the idea of the innovation but who focus on the content of their subject areas and not on such techniques as assessment. These are the pragmatists, who are less willing to take risks and make up the next 34 percent of the population.

Late majority, those who will adopt an innovation once it has become well established among the majority. These are the conservatives and skeptics, the ones with a high aversion to risk and who make up the next 34 percent of the population.

Laggards, those most likely never to adopt the innovation at all. These are the antagonists, who may even object to the innovation's use by others. They make up the last 16 percent of the population (Geoghegan, 1994, based on Moore, 1991).

Leaders must be aware that "there are transition points throughout this process, as the innovation passes from each adopter group to the next; and there are reasons for its progress to stall at almost any point" (Geoghegan, 1994, p. 12). Of these transitions, "the passage from the visionary group (the early adopters) to the mainstream is where the most significant potential for failure lies" (Geoghegan, 1994, p. 12). There is a chasm, illustrated in Figure 1.1, that often separates early adopters from the majority. If this chasm is not crossed, the innovation will remain with only about 15 percent of the population. The reasons behind this chasm have to do with the criteria used for deciding whether or not to adopt an innovation.

In order to bridge this chasm, it is important to understand the following contrasts between early adopters and the early majority (Geoghegan, 1994, p. 14):

Early Adopters	Early Majority
Favor revolutionary change	Favor evolutionary change
Visionary	Pragmatic
Project oriented	Process oriented
Risk takers	Risk averse
Willing to experiment	Want proven practices
Generally self-sufficient	May need significant support
Horizontally connected	Vertically connected

The way an innovation is presented to people in these two groups should take into account their differences. Early adopters are often intrinsically motivated to become involved in new ideas and projects because they see beyond the present and are not afraid of failure. Therefore, they tend to require little in the way of external support and to take the initiative in forming their own networks with others interested in an innovation. As a result of their energy and enthusiasm, the early adoption of an innovation may be quite promising.

Given the typical enthusiasm that is generated by early adopters, leaders can become discouraged or disenchanted with an innovation when they attempt to engage the majority. These people may not be hostile to the innovation and may even welcome it. However, the terms under which it will be successful among those in this group are quite different from the terms needed to engage the early adopters. It is those in the early majority who will be most sensitive to the potential disadvantages of assessment as a innovation, which,

**Figure 1.1. Chasm Between the Early Market
and the Mainstream Market**

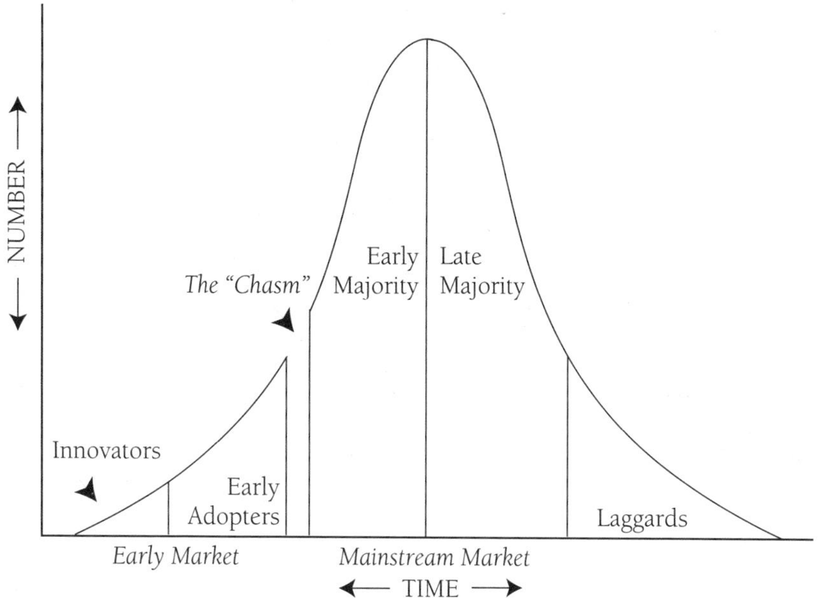

Source: Geoghegan, 1994; adapted from Moore, 1991.

as noted above, are low relative advantage, low compatibility, low flexibility, low communicability, and high complexity. They want proven practices that build on current processes so as to minimize risk. They look to central administrators and local opinion leaders within the hierarchy of the institution for guidance and confirmation of the innovation's worth. And they need more support than do early adopters because they take a pragmatic approach to change, realizing that there always are costs associated with it.

The best way to engage the majority of faculty members is to allow them to have a high degree of input into the change process. In this regard, faculty input or participation should blur distinctions that can be labeled as top-down or bottom-up. This approach emphasizes the need to mesh or blend the roles assumed by faculty, administrators, and other leaders when they collaborate in the process of change.

The time line for the change process must be long enough for the assessment to permeate all aspects of the campus culture with structures that make assessment self-sustaining. The change process should provide the necessary structures, including education to inform and orient people to assessment so that they can come to understand its meaning and its impact on their teaching. Training should be offered so that people feel prepared to manage the process and day-to-day tasks related to assessment, such as developing clear statements of student-learning outcomes, designing and implementing appropriate assessment methods, and using assessment information to improve instruction.

The change process also should help people appreciate the impact of assessment, which is likely to be the incremental improvement of instruction and enhancement of student learning. In other words, the expectation of assessment's impact that is communicated should not be immediate dramatic change but rather gradual and continual improvement. The well-planned change process will provide opportunities for those in the majority to collaborate and cooperate with others in their departments and across campus so that they can learn from one another and can identify ways to integrate their uses of assessment. Once assessment has permeated all aspects of the campus culture, people should be provided with the means to assess the process, the tasks, and the impact of assessment and then be given the opportunity to make improvements or to find an even better alternative. The only way to reach this point is to bring each individual faculty member and each faculty group through the stages of concern and the levels of use.

On many campuses, assessment may have reached the saturation point with early adopters and may be stuck and unable to span the chasm to the majority. National and local advocates for assessment, who have voiced frustration over the process and the impact of assessment, may be among the innovators and early adopter populations who do not understand the types of support needed by the majority.

Sometimes "the 'overall disruptiveness' of early adopter visionaries can alienate and anger the mainstream" (Geoghegan, 1994, p. 17, quoting Moore, 1991). This can occur because of the considerable attention that innovators and early adopters attract and because of what may be perceived by those in the majority as unreasonably high expectations created by early adopters, which the majority feels unable to meet.

Alienation also can occur because the high-visibility projects of early adopters absorb most of the available resources and leave little or nothing for others. In fact, sometimes such "start-up" funds are the only resources available for innovations such as assessment. It may be that no additional funds are allocated to support an innovation's adoption by the majority, which is more complex and time-consuming than is the case with early adopters, who are generally self-sufficient. It is counterproductive to ignore the support needed by mainstream adopters and the related resources that may be necessitated by the unanticipated and possibly disruptive side effects that occur when an innovation is spread to the mainstream.

It is up to leaders in each institution, each school or college, and each department or program to identify accurately the faculty in the broad early adopter and majority groups and to work with them over time to adapt assessment to local conditions in a way that overcomes any perceived disadvantages, which, as discussed above, may include low relative advantage over existing ways of getting student feedback and improving instruction, low compatibility with the culture and practices of higher education, low flexibility as implied by the strong emphasis on the measurement of student-learning outcomes, low communicability due to the incremental nature of improvement over a long period of time, and the high complexity that assessment seems to add to the already difficult task of teaching.

The cases represented by the institutions in this sourcebook show how, with leadership and a well-planned change process, assessment can be adapted to local conditions in a way that overcomes these potential disadvantages.

Note

1. For further detail on the sources cited in the extracted list, see Curry, 1992.

References

Curry, B. K. *Instituting Enduring Innovations: Achieving Continuity of Change in Higher Education.* ASHE-ERIC Higher Education Report, no. 7. Washington, D.C.: School of Education and Human Development, George Washington University, 1992.

Geoghegan, W. H. "What Ever Happened to Instructional Technology?" In S. Bapna, A. Emdad, and J. Zaveri (eds.), *Proceedings of the 22nd Annual Conference of the International Business Schools Computing Association.* Baltimore: International Business Schools Computing Association, 1994.

Geoghegan, W. H. "Instructional Technology and the Mainstream: The Risks of Success." Maytum Distinguished Lecture. Fredonia: State University of New York College at Fredonia, Oct. 23, 1996. (Forthcoming as a chapter in S. Rush and D. Oblinger [eds.], *The Future Compatible Campus.* Boston: Ankor, 1997.)

Hall, G. E., George, A. A., and Rutherford, W. L. *Measuring Stages of Concern About the Innovation: A Manual for Use of the SoC Questionnaire.* (2nd ed.) Austin: Research and Development Center for Teacher Education, University of Texas, 1979.

Hall, G. E., Loucks, S. F., Rutherford, W. L., and Newlove, B. W. "Levels of Use of the Innovation: A Framework for Analyzing Innovation Adoption." *Journal of Teacher Education,* 1975, *26* (1).

Hall, G. E., Wallace, R. C., Jr., and Dossett, W. A. *A Developmental Conceptualization of the Adoption Process Within Educational Institutions.* Austin: Research and Development Center for Teacher Education, University of Texas, 1973.

Moore, G. A. *Crossing the Chasm: Marketing and Selling Technology Products to Mainstream Customers.* New York: Harper Business, 1991.

Newlove, B. W., and Hall, G. E. *A Manual for Assessing Open-Ended Statements of Concern About an Innovation.* Austin: Research and Development Center for Teacher Education, University of Texas, 1976 (no. 3029). (ED 144 207)

Palmer, P. J. "Good Talk About Good Teaching: Improving Teaching Through Conversation and Community." *Change,* 1993, *25* (6).

Rogers, E. M. "The Communications of Innovations in a Complex Institution." *Educational Record,* Winter 1968, pp. 67–77.

Rogers, E. M. *Diffusion of Innovations.* New York: Free Press, 1995.

PETER J. GRAY *is associate director, Center for Instructional Development, Syracuse University.*

Is a successful assessment program principally a question of technique or institutional culture? At Truman State University, an initially modest commitment to improved student learning transformed an institution and influenced a national movement.

The Right Idea at the Right Time: Development of a Transformational Assessment Culture

Jack Magruder, Michael A. McManis, Candace C. Young

Assessment can have a profound transformational impact on an institution. For this result to occur, however, such core values as the improvement of student learning through the systematic collection of performance-related data and information must become integrated into the institution's culture. Successful assessment is much more than techniques, processes, or even outcomes; it is a cultural issue that affects how a community of scholars defines its work and its responsibilities to its students. Significantly, the culture of assessment is typically a somewhat unstable arrangement, which requires continual nurture and support even at an institution with undergraduate education at the heart of its mission. A vigorous assessment program will require the faculty to step outside the security of their disciplines or departments, to view student learning from a holistic perspective, and to accept collective responsibility for the success of their institution's educational program. In the contemporary academy, this level of commitment is neither easy to initiate nor easy to sustain. Yet, the rewards for success can be enormous for both faculty and students. This is the story of one institution's effort to address these difficult issues.

Beginnings of Assessment

Truman State University, formerly Northeast Missouri State University, initiated its assessment program soon after a new president, Charles J. McClain, assumed office in 1970 and brought to the campus a desire for quality education. Furthermore, he insisted that the university should be able to measure its positive impact on students. McClain and his new dean of instruction, Darrell W. Krueger, worked throughout the 1970s to increase the university's focus on the quality of student learning. In fact, an initiative that began as a simple assessment program gradually evolved into a new institutional culture that transformed the university. Over a period of several years, McClain, Krueger, and the faculty established an assessment system that was instrumental in developing an impressive university-wide emphasis on student learning. Eventually, the demonstrable improvements in the quality of its programs and the academic achievements of its students attracted the attention of the state coordinating board, the legislature, and even the national media. In 1985, as part of a coordinating-board strategy to encourage all public institutions to focus their missions and to place more emphasis on qualitative improvement, the Missouri General Assembly passed legislation designating the university as the public liberal arts and sciences university for the state. More recently, independent national rankings have become popular, and Truman has frequently been cited as a national education leader in terms of relative cost and quality. After twenty-five years, the university's achievements have far exceeded anyone's expectations when the odyssey began. Were these accomplishments the product of good fortune, or shrewd leadership and much hard work, or a combination of these factors? What lessons might other institutions learn from the Truman experience?

Stimulus. McClain was the primary stimulus for Truman State University's assessment program, but his goals were much larger than just building an assessment program. In the early 1970s, it would be at least a decade before institutional accountability for student performance became a national issue. Yet, McClain brought to the presidency a belief that the university had an obligation to provide its students an education that would prepare them to be highly competitive in graduate or professional school and employment. He stimulated the campus community to think about these issues by inquiring how well the university was accomplishing this goal. As part of this process, McClain asked many questions that faculty found difficult to answer effectively. For example, how do we know that the university's programs are of high quality? How do we know that we are making a positive difference for our students? Are our graduates in all disciplines proficient in mathematical, writing, and speaking skills? Do they have a working knowledge of history, literature, science, and the arts? Are our graduates competitive with graduates from the best universities in the country? If so, how do we know this?

Another significant factor during the early years of McClain's presidency was a transition in the university's mission from a regional state teachers' college to a regional comprehensive university. McClain believed that as a teachers' college, the university had access to excellent feedback on the quality of its programs: "Faculty and staff could verify how well they were doing by the placement of graduates, and by the intimate working relationship that the college had developed with the public schools and regional superintendents" (McClain and Krueger, 1985, p. 33).

With the expanded mission, however, demonstrating the quality of numerous new programs was much more challenging and problematic. After reviewing the data for graduates who were trying to pursue graduate and professional degrees, the president believed there was cause for concern. McClain was impressed with the British education system's use of tutorials followed by examinations prepared by external examiners. By analogy, he thought that the faculty at regional public universities such as Truman could play the role of mentor or coach by preparing students to achieve nationally competitive knowledge and skill outcomes. On completion of a student's program, one measure of achievement would be an external national examination written by top professionals in the major field. Such an approach would provide objective evidence to students, faculty, parents, and state leaders of institutional quality that would be much more persuasive than the generalized rhetorical assurances commonly offered by many institutions.

Charge. As a first step in the implementation of this vision of performance assessment, McClain wrote to all graduating seniors in the 1972–73 school year offering them the opportunity to take a nationally standardized examination as an additional measure of their level of mastery in their major. For the first few years, participation by graduating students remained voluntary. Meanwhile, faculty were asked to review examinations and to choose the ones they thought were most appropriate for assessing knowledge in the major field. In 1975, recognizing that multiple measures of assessment were necessary to create an accurate picture of institutional performance, Truman State introduced surveys of students' satisfaction with academic and personal achievement and started a program of general education value-added testing of students. Faculty also began to develop numerous local instruments for assessing student learning in and out of the classroom. Over the following two decades, faculty have conducted a continual search for the best mixture of assessment instruments—national and local, qualitative and objective—that would provide the university with multiple, appropriate measures of students' knowledge, skills, and attitudes.

Logistics. By deliberately fostering a collegial, low-risk environment, McClain and Krueger were able to persuade faculty that they were sincere in their efforts to create an improved university and that faculty had nothing to fear from the assessment system. The trust that was developed between the faculty and the administration provided the necessary support for the enterprise. Because the leadership implemented assessment slowly and because they continually reassured faculty that the data would not be used punitively, they were successful in establishing the environment necessary for their emphasis on improving student learning to be embraced campuswide. Assessment was presented to the faculty and was perceived by them as a way to monitor progress toward student-learning goals. A particularly useful strategy that McClain and Krueger used to keep assessment issues before the faculty in nonthreatening ways was their impromptu hallway inquiries in which they would ask faculty such questions as, "What do you think happened to John Doe? He had an exceptional GPA but scored only at the twenty-fifth percentile on his senior exam." Without this focus on lofty quality goals, assessment might have been rejected by faculty as an intrusion intended to evaluate *them*.

Methods of data distribution also facilitated a low-threat environment. Faculty received annual and historical data on their majors along with university-wide averages and national norms whenever they were available. Faculty did not receive comparative cross-campus data by major or faculty member. The dean of instruction's office was the primary facilitator of data distribution and use. Although the university's testing office administered the examinations, no central assessment office was established, as both the president and the dean felt such an office would actually reduce faculty ownership and analysis of the data. Instead, the president and the dean created numerous occasions for faculty to analyze the data publicly at university workshops, planning retreats, and board of governors meetings. Moreover, the president and the dean were role models in the use of assessment data, as it was routinely part of their analyses regarding the strengths and weaknesses of the campus, future goals for the university, and new program initiatives.

Initial Activities

Faculty grew accustomed to the president's and the dean's constant references to student-learning goals. This consistent message meant that faculty, staff, and administrators knew with unusual clarity what was valued. Furthermore, the campus culture gradually embraced assessment as a way to produce multiple data points that would provide basic evidence for discussions on university interests and issues as well as for university reporting to accreditation and state agencies. In addition to these university-wide assessment purposes, individual disciplines learned to use the assessment program and its attendant culture to develop discipline-specific evaluations, including five-year program reviews.

Implementation Stages. As noted previously, the first stage of the assessment process at Truman relied on nationally standardized examinations and locally developed surveys. By 1980, the university had an assessment system that required all students to take a nationally normed pre-and posttest of general education, to pass a local writing assessment, to complete three student surveys, and to take a nationally normed examination in the major. It should be noted that only the sophomore-year writing assessment directly affected a student's progress toward a degree, by requiring a minimum score. Just as assessment was implemented in a nonpunitive fashion with respect to faculty, the same principle was applied to students. Unless external licensure requirements prescribed a particular level of performance, students were required only to complete a given assessment process rather than to attain a specified minimum score.

By 1990, several other assessment methods were added to complement existing instruments with more qualitative assessments and student self-assessment. Several of the new instruments reflected the 1985 change in the university's mission to the state's public liberal arts and sciences university. For example, as part of this mission change, the faculty senate adopted a requirement for capstone experiences in the major. Faculty at the discipline level have often used this capstone experience to implement major-specific assessments—that is, a major may require its students to write a thesis, to present research, to interview with faculty from the discipline, or to sit for a local comprehensive examination. The faculty senate also encouraged each discipline to participate in a portfolio assessment of student-learning outcomes associated with the liberal arts and sciences mission. In 1992, an annual interview project was begun to permit more in-depth investigation of specific university issues, such as factors affecting a successful transition from high school to college for first-time freshmen. These various initiatives were direct attempts by the institution to assess the student-learning process as broadly as possible and to develop multiple measures of institutional performance.

One unique aspect of the university's assessment program is that every student participates in assessment. This practice derives from the premise that each individual student should be able to use assessment results. If only a sample of students were used, a message would be suggested that assessment is strictly for university and accountability purposes and is not directly relevant to students. Truman State University encourages students to use assessment information for self-evaluation, and each adviser is expected to review data reports with advisees. If, for example, students are weak in mathematics, they should be encouraged by the adviser to take extra course work to correct the weakness. Conversely, if students have high levels of achievement, they should be advised to select a higher-level, more challenging course. Advisees are sometimes so swayed by the improvement in their general education posttest scores that they begin to think of their future differently. It has been the institution's experience that sustaining a student-centered focus in the assessment program has been a critical element in continuing student support and participation in the process.

Findings and Actions: What Worked. After nearly twenty-five years of assessment of student learning at Truman, opinions of its significance vary. Truman has discovered that assessment data alone are a necessary but not always sufficient component of the institutional change process for a university. Equally important for Truman has been establishing a campus culture that not only embraces assessment conceptually but also actively supports organizational self-evaluation and the desire for improvement. Four factors were essential in building this culture—the leadership's clarity and driving commitment, the timing and motivation for the assessment initiative, the integration of assessment into university processes from program review and accreditation to planning and committee work, and the reliance on faculty to develop and implement assessment.

The first of these factors has been described above and needs no further discussion other than to add that the passionate commitment of the organization's leaders to clearly expressed goals was contagious. Talent development and the pursuit of excellence are values close to the heart of most educators, but change often involves risk and uncertainty, which leads to resistance. Strong organizational leadership is essential if the natural conservatism, autonomy, and inertia of the academy are to be overcome.

A second factor that contributed to the development of a campus culture focused on quality improvement and assessment was the timing of the initiatives. The development of an assessment program in the early 1970s that featured objective measures of quality in effect anticipated the accountability movement of the 1980s. The fact that several national reports were published in the mid-1980s that condemned a perceived decline in educational standards and called for systematic assessment of student learning, notably A Nation at Risk and Involvement in Learning (National Commission on Excellence in Education, 1983; National Institute of Education, 1984), helped reinforce the cultural ethos at Truman—that student learning needed to be improved and that assessment could help monitor progress toward that end. The national attention given these reports legitimated the university's pioneering efforts in assessment and continual improvement.

In 1984, these national concerns provided the foundation that led to the university receiving the G. Theodore Mitau Award for Innovation and Excellence from the American Association of State Colleges and Universities. This award culminated in the production of a film on the institution's assessment program and a book, In Pursuit of Degrees with Integrity (Northeast Missouri State University, 1984a). The changes that had been implemented at the university by the early 1980s positioned the university to capitalize on the state of Missouri's interest in diversifying the structure of its higher education system by creating a public liberal arts and sciences university. The university's reputation also benefited in the mid-1980s when the governor of Missouri, John Ashcroft, was commissioned to chair a task force on college quality for the National Governors' Association, and the subsequent report, Time for Results (Task Force on College Quality, 1986), drew on the institution's experiences. As an early adopter of assessment processes, Truman was able to avoid the divisive effects of an externally mandated assessment requirement while reaping the benefits that accrue to an institution that can successfully anticipate and respond to major environmental changes.

While support for assessment from both institutional leaders and external decision makers was crucial, it was not enough. One of the most salient factors for the successful implementation of the university's assessment culture was the actual integration of the results of the assessment program into the management and operation of the institution. Unless faculty and students can see evidence that the results of their assessment efforts actually make a substantive difference in their work, it is very difficult to move beyond a potentially cynical compliance mode of operation. Consequently, as the university developed its longitudinal assessment database, the president's and vice president's expectations for its use in campus processes increased. When the university was conducting its accreditation self-study in the early 1980s, assessment data were used whenever they applied to the accreditation criteria and questions. This was a very influential decision because approximately 25 percent of the faculty were involved in the various committees that wrote the report. Similarly, as the state instituted a requirement for cyclical program reviews, the university integrated assessment data into the report format. Each discipline must now use assessment data for program review and other reporting activities and presentations. Planning committees, governance councils, and faculty development processes have each been connected with assessment data and processes.

More specifically, the university has found the data extraordinarily helpful in raising red flags, thereby placing issues on the university's discussion agenda. Data implications are especially effective if several different assessment methods suggest problems in the same area. In these instances, university discussion can move more quickly beyond the question of whether a university weakness exists to an exploration of ideas for improvement. Among the many improvements that have been made on the basis of the assessment data have been the strengthening of the general education mathematics and science requirements, based on low value-added test scores; the implementation of a writing-across-the-curriculum requirement, based on disappointing improvements in student writing skills; and the increased expectations for student time on task through enhanced course requirements, based on student survey reports and assessment test results in the major. Results such as these, rather than the completion of compliance reports to central state officials, make assessment programs real and vital for faculty.

Truman State University has benefited enormously from having administrators and faculty who have embraced challenges and change. Its top leaders have been gifted in planting ideas for improvement and in empowering faculty and staff to develop, refine, and modify them. The two most significant distinguishing features of Truman's assessment program have been the integration of its results into the management of the institution as described above and its high level of reliance on faculty for its development and implementation. Over the years, the various programs and disciplines supported by the university have developed different cultures of use, but all faculty are aware of the assessment system and the data it generates—in part through their own involvement in the process. In addition to using assessment data for program reviews and other reporting activities, approximately 20 percent of the faculty have participated as portfolio readers for the liberal arts and sciences portfolio evaluation or as readers for the university-wide sophomore writing assessment. Though it is not unanimous, faculty support for and interest in assessment is unusually strong. For example, a faculty survey in the early 1980s showed that 70 percent thought assessment contributed to curricular improvement (Northeast Missouri State University, 1984b). More recently, in a 1996 survey of public universities in Missouri by the Coordinating Board for Higher Education, faculty at Truman State University more strongly supported assessment and performance-based funding than did faculty at other public four-year institutions (Missouri Department of Higher Education, 1996).

One result of this very high level of faculty support and involvement in the assessment program has been successful university initiatives, which have reached the core of the student-learning process; for example, increased faculty-student interaction, heightened expectations for student achievement, and enhanced student involvement in the learning process. Specific examples of these successes include increases in the number of "learning communities" in which faculty and students learn outside the classroom, the time students spend studying for classes, the percent of students going on to graduate and professional school, and the number of small introductory classes that encourage students to become more involved in their learning. Reviews of assessment results and corresponding transcript analyses have caused many of the discipline faculties to rewrite requirements, to establish a clearer rationale for the sequencing of course work, and to strengthen expectations that students learn the breadth of their majors. Several disciplines have also integrated specific skill development activities into required courses in the major so that all students graduating in a discipline have several opportunities to practice particular kinds of writing, speaking, analysis, and other skills. The curriculum for the liberal studies program at the university has been systematically upgraded in terms of its ability to challenge students and to foster the development of higher-level cognitive skills. Other initiatives at the university that have evolved from the focus on quality and assessment include the development of a very extensive undergraduate research program, a freshman transition program, and residential colleges to facilitate a more scholarly living-learning environment. Without the consistent involvement in, and ownership of, the assessment program by the faculty over an extended period of time, these achievements would not have been possible.

Subsequent Signs of Progress and Problems

Assessment as a distinct, separable institutional activity has limited potential to effect improvement. As the previous discussion has shown, the extent to which assessment is connected to important university decisions and leadership priorities is positively associated with its potential contribution to the campus. As one might surmise, the ebb and flow pattern of campus agendas provides challenges and opportunities for an assessment system's effectiveness.

Additional Factors Facilitating Progress. Although each of the primary factors influencing the development of assessment at Truman that were outlined previously was essential to our success, it is difficult to overstate the importance of the leadership provided by the president and the chief academic officer. Furthermore, a significant component of their success was their longevity in office: McClain served nineteen years and Krueger served sixteen years. Together, they were able to gain and keep the trust of the faculty over an extended period. This was due in large part to the fact that their ideas placed academics at the center of the institution's mission: instruction and student learning were the campus's dominant priorities. McClain and Krueger were also extremely disciplined in keeping the agenda focused and not permitting other issues to displace the attention given to the university's central purposes. Individual members of the faculty, staff, and administration may have disagreed with the leaders at times, but the overarching goals of the university were clear. Furthermore, by the early 1980s most faculty not only supported the overarching goals, but they also supported the use of assessment to measure them.

Part of the successful strategy used by McClain and Krueger was to assure that good things happened because of assessment—particularly as it was linked to the management of the institution and as faculty were encouraged to take ownership. As faculty became involved in improvement efforts, they received verbal and written recognition. Over time, the students admitted to the university were better prepared, and the university's academic reputation increased, thereby attracting the attention of ever larger numbers of highly prepared students. It was a matter of institutional policy that the university did not seek direct state support to establish or maintain its assessment program. Rather, the institution used the results of the assessment program to provide benchmark data and evidence in support of specific proposals to improve student learning or to remedy documented weaknesses. The first example of this strategy occurred in 1979 when the institution received more than $400,000 for targeted improvements in four discipline areas—language and literature, science, mathematics, and business. Similarly, the university received a state appropriation in the mid-1980s for the renovation and expansion of its library, in part as a result of longitudinal survey data showing a decline in student satisfaction with library facilities. Faculty could, in addition, see the results of curricular changes that had been stimulated by assessment data and the resulting conversations and decisions. Ultimately, the university's selection by the state coordinating board and the general assembly in 1985 to become a selective, statewide, liberal arts and sciences university must be attributed to the university's long march toward quality and measured accountability.

Significantly, just as important as having good things happen because of the assessment program was the assurance faculty, staff, and students received that assessment data would never be used punitively. All the fears of high-stakes decisions being made because of assessment data did not come true. Data were the beginning point for evaluation of programmatic strengths and weaknesses. Dialogue and consideration of improvement initiatives were the activities faculty and staff experienced and observed. Faculty and staff evaluations were never linked to the assessment program, and coercion to participate in the program was avoided.

In addition to benefiting from effective internal institutional leadership that successfully identified a variety of ways to make assessment attractive and meaningful to the faculty and students, assessment at Truman benefited greatly from a very positive external environment that reinforced and rewarded the effort. The institution had the good fortune of initiating the program prior to the promulgation of assessment requirements by external agencies, such as state officials or accrediting agencies, which can exacerbate faculty concerns about intrusion and improper use of data. Similarly, the public policy environment in Missouri has also been very synergistic with Truman's effort—providing crucial support and rewards. For example, a state initiative in the 1990s to differentiate the public four-year institutions in terms of clientele served has been invaluable in legitimating the institution's decision to increase the selectivity of its student body. The state coordinating board's decision to embrace a performance funding component in its funding-formula recommendations has similarly reinforced the institution's commitment to quality enhancement.

A key question for other institutions evaluating the Truman experience as a possible model for their own efforts is whether the advantages of leadership and the state policy environment have rendered the Truman experience unique. On balance, we think not. No single leadership style will be best for every institution. In addition, though the positive external environment has helped foster—and in some ways facilitate—the development of the new culture, the essential outlines of the new culture were in place before the outside world was very aware of the assessment program. External policymakers can create an environment friendly to assessment and quality improvement, but ultimately, it is the academic community that must create and sustain the program.

Problems Blocking Progress to Date. Truman's assessment program has faced several obstacles since its inception, but the most important among them has been socializing large numbers of new members into the university community and its culture of assessment. The successful incorporation of new members into the culture of a community is a challenge for all organizations. However, when the organization has learned to prioritize values that are quite unique, its socialization challenges are heightened. More attention must be given toward consciously integrating new students, faculty, and staff to the values that support the atypical practices of the institution—in this case, numerous quality initiatives and assessment.

The magnitude of student turnover is easy to describe and easy to underestimate. Having positive student support for assessment in one time frame evaporates rather quickly. Significantly, much the same can be true of faculty. Although faculty turnover is much less dramatic than that for students, over a five-year period it can be quite significant—particularly in disciplines that are growing or in disciplines affected by retirements. It is easy to forget that there needs to be an ongoing effort to inform affected publics of the rationale and benefits of the assessment system.

As it is in most other organizations, a change in leadership can be extremely stressful. Because effective and consistent leadership is vital in the linking of university goals to meaningful assessments, new leadership can unintentionally undermine the system. New leaders have to be socialized to understand and use the data. The temptation for leaders to delegate the assessment processes to others can quickly make assessment just one more report to read. Institutionalization of the process—for example, the establishment of an office, a director, and annual reports—may be sufficient to demonstrate an assessment system, but this type of a compliance model cannot equal the impact potential of assessment that is actually incorporated into the culture and used by leadership as the conscious foundation for many institutional decisions.

It is Truman's experience that even with extensive experience and broad acceptance, the culture of assessment and quality improvement can be very fragile and still requires constant nurturing and care. Even at a teaching institution such as Truman, the traditional pressures of academe to focus on your discipline, or on your research, or on your majors, rather than on the university as a whole or on the teaching-learning process broadly understood are very strong pressures indeed. In the final analysis, assessment is a community activity that views educational processes holistically. In the highly individualistic, departmentalized world of the modern academy, it must be continually fostered and supported.

Looking Ahead. The university recognizes that the problems identified above are concerns that must be addressed in ways that will reinforce quality goals and continual institutional improvement. Finding ways to keep this message vital is the challenge for leaders at all levels and in all units of the university. The leadership must also make sure that the assessment data that are gathered remain consistent with university goals and continue to be used to inform university decision making. If the leaders of the organization do not use the data, who will? Lack of use by leaders is a quick way to devalue the importance of assessment for everyone else in the organization, especially students.

A related concern at Truman is to prepare the next generation of institutional leaders, who must soon assume responsibility for the future of the assessment culture. The majority of the founding generation of faculty and administrative leaders, who have been responsible for the remarkable development of the assessment culture at Truman, have either left the institution to pursue other career opportunities or will be eligible to retire in the next five to eight years. Given the distinctive culture that is required truly to support and nurture a comprehensive assessment program, great care is needed in developing new leadership internally and in acculturating new leadership recruited external to the institution. Preparing for this imminent transition is one of our key challenges as an academic community.

A key future challenge at a more technical level is to establish the validity and reliability of the university's qualitative assessment instruments. For most goals, several forms of assessment data exist. When multiple measures suggest conclusions in common, the assessment results can be viewed as more reliable. However, in order for university measures on qualitative assessments to be valid in a longitudinal planning process, it is important to know that the measure is reliable. Otherwise, documenting improvement over time is not really possible. To report that 65 percent of students submitted quality interdisciplinary portfolio entries in contrast to 50 percent the year before assumes inter-reader reliability. The process of developing inter-reader reliability is a significant undertaking. Once achieved, though, the ability to report the results of qualitative instruments in a meaningful way to people who were not part of the assessment scoring process improves dramatically.

Conclusion

Profound changes at this university over the last twenty-five years have enabled it to achieve results far beyond anyone's expectations. Though Truman started with an effort that was initially as modest in scope as it was audacious in its vision, it has developed a culture of assessment that has served its students and faculty—as well as the citizens of its state—very well. As the state sought more refined missions for its universities, Truman was chosen to be the selective, statewide public liberal arts and sciences university. Some have suggested that the university's acceptance of accountability matched the legislative and state culture of "show me." After the successful implementation of the mission change, the state recently renamed the institution Truman State University. National magazines, college guides, and higher education experts now almost routinely cite the spectacular and planned improvement of the university. To quote Peter Ewell, a national expert on assessment and presently a member of Truman's board of governors, in an oral report to the board in November 1991, "The experience that this university has had is astonishing in terms of the amount of change which has occurred in a small period of time. I know personally of no other institution—and I work with about 120 at this point—which has changed so much, so consciously, so single-mindedly and so successfully."

It is hard to argue with assessment when it is so closely tied to such good things happening to a university. It is a path that we heartily recommend to our colleagues across the nation.

References

McClain, C., and Krueger, D. "Using Outcomes Assessment: A Case Study in Institutional Change." In P. T. Ewell (ed.), *Assessing Educational Outcomes*. New Directions for Institutional Research, no. 47. San Francisco: Jossey-Bass, 1985.

Missouri Department of Higher Education. *1996 Statewide Funding for Results Survey*. Jefferson City, Mo.: Coordinating Board for Higher Education, May 1996.

National Commission on Excellence in Education. *A Nation at Risk*. Washington, D.C.: U.S. Government Printing Office, 1983.

National Institute of Education. *Involvement in Learning: Realizing the Potential of American Higher Education*. Washington, D.C.: U.S. Department of Education, 1984.

Northeast Missouri State University. *In Pursuit of Degrees with Integrity: A Value-Added Approach to Undergraduate Assessment*. Washington, D.C.: American Association of State Colleges and Universities, 1984a.

Northeast Missouri State University. *1984 Faculty Survey*. Kirksville: Northeast Missouri State University, 1984b.

Task Force on College Quality. *Time for Results: The Governors' 1991 Report on Education.* Washington, D.C.: National Governors' Association Center for Policy Research and Analysis, Aug. 1986.

JACK MAGRUDER is professor of chemistry and president, Truman State University. He was previously head of the science division and vice president for academic affairs.

MICHAEL A. MCMANIS is dean of planning and institutional development, Truman State University. Previously, he was with the Missouri Coordinating Board for Higher Education, where for several years, he served as chief academic and planning officer.

CANDACE C. YOUNG is professor of political science and president of the faculty senate, Truman State University. She has consulted extensively on assessment at other institutions.

This chapter contains a review of academic assessment at Ball State University. It describes areas of strength and continuing challenges to assessing academic programs.

Assessment at Ball State University

Catherine A. Palomba

This chapter contains an overview of Ball State University's academic assessment program. It traces our beginnings, reviews our present, and anticipates our future. Several current assessment activities are described. In addition, areas of strength in our assessment program and challenges to conducting successful assessment are presented.

Getting Started

Under the leadership of John Worthen, president of Ball State University since 1984, the university has developed a clear vision of its role and mission. The view of Ball State as a premier teaching university with emphasis on undergraduate education and select graduate programs has become widely held across campus. Ball State now emphasizes its advantages as a midsize university, which offers more varied academic programs than a small liberal arts college and at the same time provides a range of personalized educational experiences that might not be found at a large research university. With about seventeen thousand undergraduate and two thousand graduate students in seven colleges, Ball State takes pride in its strong academic and cocurricular programs. Consistent with its renewed commitment to excellence, in 1986, Ball State's mission statement was amended to call for "constant and vigorous self-assessment."

At the same time that the university was reexamining its overall role and mission, the university's general studies program was undergoing substantial revision. The original cafeteria-style design was revised to include a forty-one credit-hour program with limited distribution options and a core of five specific courses. All undergraduates, regardless of college, now participate in the same general education curriculum. An important element of the redesigned program was a requirement calling for assessment activities. Each department would now be asked to demonstrate that its general studies courses were meeting the program's newly articulated goals and objectives.

With a common view of the university's mission and a firm commitment to undertaking assessment, the university was ready to respond to the state legislature's request for proposals to create an institutional program of academic assessment. In fact, Ball State was the only university that responded to the legislature's request. In spring 1987, the university submitted a proposal for a multifaceted program of "excellence in education." The proposal included a request for funding of a central assessment office with an administrative staff who would focus on standardized testing and other assessment activities. As a result of the proposal, the Office of Academic Assessment was founded in July 1987. This office works in parallel with the university's Office of Institutional Research and reports to the associate provost. The office has four professionals engaged in assessment. Funding was also provided by the state legislature for assessment projects, including testing, faculty support, graduate assistants, and assessment-related travel.

Early Approach and Activities

With a newly created office but no state-mandated reporting requirements, initial activities focused on assessment of general studies and collection of institutional data. An attempt was also made to introduce assessment to the disciplines. Travel funds were provided to departments so that faculty members could attend regional and national assessment conferences. Professionals from the Office of Academic Assessment consulted with several departments that were exploring assessment activities. It was recognized, however, that assessment was a new concept at the university and that departments would need some time to become familiar with and accept the value of assessment.

By year's end, the office had experimented with several national comprehensive examinations for general studies, including the American College Test's College Outcomes Measure Program (ACT COMP) Objective Test and the Academic Profile. A number of departments used the Student Goals Exploration Survey available through the National Center for Research to Improve Postsecondary Teaching and Learning. This instrument allowed teachers to determine learning goals for students in general education classrooms. In addition, six departments began to use major-field examinations available through the Educational Testing Service.

The assessment office quickly moved beyond the emphasis on value-added assessment, which had been so prominent in the initial funding proposal. Focus shifted to a more comprehensive approach to assessing the educational environment and its impact on students.

After a period of exploration, and in anticipation of a reaccreditation visit from the North Central Association of Colleges and Schools, the administration realized that the university's program of assessment needed to become formalized through a set of written materials. The roles of various constituencies needed to be articulated, and the concepts and ideas of assessment needed to be supported throughout the institution.

In fall 1991, Warren Vander Hill, provost and vice president for academic affairs, issued a statement that clarified and reinforced the role of academic assessment at the university. As described in the statement, the overall goals of Ball State's academic assessment program are to evaluate academic programs and to enhance student learning. The statement highlights the opportunities that assessment provides to demonstrate the university's strengths as well as to identify areas for growth and improvement. It sets forth the expectation that all colleges, schools, and departments will participate in assessment activities and use the results to stimulate program improvement. Faculty, administrators, and students are expected to work together to accomplish assessment goals. Alumni and community representatives also have a role to play in providing information and support for assessment activities.

The Provost's Statement articulates six major assessment objectives that have guided the activities of the program. These include determining the knowledge and attitudes of students when they enter the university, when they complete the general studies program, and when they finish their majors. Other objectives include determining the factors that contribute to program completion, determining students' satisfaction with their educational experiences, and assessing students' success in employment and further education.

Soon after the Provost's Statement was issued, an initial draft of the university's Academic Assessment Plan was prepared by the director of assessment. The draft combined the principles of the Provost's Statement with a description of the existing assessment program. The draft document was then circulated to the assessment office's advisory committee and to university administrators and faculty. With modifications, the plan (Ball State University, 1992) was submitted to representatives of the North Central Association of Colleges and Schools when they made their reaccreditation visit in fall 1993. A supplementary document describing assessment in each of the colleges and schools at the university was also prepared and made available to representatives of the North Central Association (Ball State University, 1993).

Current Activities

The Provost's Statement and the plan prepared for the North Central Association have continued to guide the assessment program. Based on the plan, each of the six objectives of the assessment program is addressed through one or more major activities. Standardized testing and surveys are used to determine the initial knowledge and attitudes of students and how these change over the course of study. Surveys are also used to determine the satisfaction and success of students at specific points during their academic experiences. Current activities fall into three broad groups—university-wide, general education, and discipline-specific assessment activities.

University-Wide Assessment. University-wide assessment activities are those that are beyond the scope of an individual college or department. These activities help address overall issues of learning that are important to the university, help the units of the university see common goals, and allow for the creation of university norms. They also allow for disaggregation of results so that discipline-specific information can be gained. At Ball State, university-wide assessment activities concentrate on learning objectives that cut across discipline lines. They address broad learning objectives, such as critical thinking, clear communication, and ability to work in groups, which appear in the university's mission statement. They also address the areas of wellness, computer competency, and experiential education that are so important at Ball State.

In order to collect university-wide data, the Office of Academic Assessment has developed a cycle of surveys that are administered at various time intervals while students are in college. Survey information is collected from students when they enter the university, at midcollege, upon graduation, and two years after graduation. These surveys have a common core of questions that focus on assessment issues. Though each survey focuses on issues relevant to the particular time frame, each also addresses issues that are common across all time periods.

Each fall, entering students are asked to complete a survey, Making Achievement Possible (MAP), which was developed at Ball State. This survey asks students for a self-assessment of their knowledge and skills and an indication of their willingness to seek help. The survey asks about college goals and life goals. Questions about initial adjustment to college, plans for participating in college activities, and likely uses of time are also included. This survey was developed jointly by the academic assessment, academic advising, and housing–residence life offices, as well as the learning center. The results of MAP are used by students, academic advisers, and residence-hall directors in planning the year's activities, programs, and services. Each student receives a personalized report based on that individual's responses to the survey and basic admissions data. The report indicates how the student compares with the overall entering class and includes recommendations about various services at Ball State. In addition, it includes an analysis of the way the student is allocating his or her time. Students who have not allocated adequate time for their studies are urged to do so. Academic advisers and residence-hall directors receive condensed versions of the students' reports. As the survey is administered on computers in campus labs, the data are readily available for report processing. As of fall 1996, the survey is available on scan forms, which also allow for quick processing.

The freshman survey data collected through MAP has been used to conduct retention studies. These studies have increased our understanding of the characteristics and behaviors that contribute to program completion. In a recent study, characteristics of students who "leave by choice" were contrasted with those of students who leave because they are disqualified. The study found that the freshmen who disqualify score lowest on survey items that reflect academic commitment, such as attending classes, expected grades, and time management skills. The freshmen who do not return by choice score lowest on survey items that reflect social fit and institutional commitment, such as expectation of graduating from Ball State, plans to participate in campus activities, and fitting in at Ball State. A freshman year experience survey has been created to follow up on some of these issues. The university has also introduced a freshman-year seminar for students who are most at risk for dropping out.

Surveys of seniors and alumni have allowed us to track the experiences, attitudes, and successes of our graduates. Both of these surveys contain a set of questions that ask respondents how well their experiences at Ball State prepared them in various areas of skills and knowledge. A three-point response scale includes the categories of *very well, satisfactorily,* and *poorly.* Both surveys ask respondents to indicate their levels of satisfaction with aspects of their academic department. The senior survey contains items about participation in campus activities, satisfaction with student services, and importance of life goals. The alumni survey asks about employment and further education. It also asks about the use of various mathematics, computer, and writing skills on the job. Results from these surveys are widely circulated. Faculty teaching English courses have been particularly interested in the information about writing on the job because they can use these results to plan writing exercises and to motivate their students by making references to the world after graduation. Results from the senior and alumni surveys about computer competency have also generated much interest.

In addition to using locally developed surveys, we have also used some nationally available surveys. We have used the College Student Experiences Questionnaire for students at the end of the freshman and sophomore years and have found the information it provides about educational activities and gains in learning to be very helpful. We also used the Student Goals Exploration Survey early in our program. This survey provided valuable information about the learning goals of students in various courses. Because questions about these goals are now incorporated in locally developed surveys, we have not continued to use this instrument.

General Education Assessment. Consistent with the proposal submitted to the state legislature, Ball State pilot tested several general studies comprehensive examinations. After a period of initial exploration, the College Basic Academic Subjects Examination was selected for use in the summer of 1989 and is still in use today. This exam was selected because it provides a variety of scores for English, mathematics, science, and social studies. It also provides scores for three levels of reasoning. The university uses this exam to study the knowledge of entering freshmen and their growth through the general studies program. All incoming freshmen are tested during orientation, and a large sample of upper-division students is tested during class sessions. Early results from this examination were very useful for mathematics faculty as they redesigned the applied mathematics course that is required of most graduates. Continued use has allowed us to track student growth and performance with respect to various general education goals.

In 1987, the university implemented a required writing competency examination for juniors, which is managed by the director of the writing competency program. Students must register for and attend a special two-hour testing session to complete their essays. They are given a prompt at the test and are graded on a three-point holistic scale. The focus of the test is on whether the student can take a position and defend it. Three-point scores are assigned to papers in which students provide solid, forceful, and polished arguments in favor of a position. Students who fail to pass the exam after two attempts are required to complete an intensive seven-week writing course.

Extensive assessment information has been collected through the recently completed five-year cycle of general studies course assessment that was initiated in fall 1991. Departments with at least one general studies course were asked to rate the university's programmatic goals for general studies and to demonstrate that each course was meeting these goals. Departments were expected to provide both cognitive and attitudinal information about students. Each department was permitted and encouraged to develop its own assessment tools. Following a predetermined calendar and a set of reporting guidelines, each department assessed its own general studies courses and prepared a report for the general studies subcommittee of the university senate. This committee reviewed all of the information and issued a set of conclusions and recommendations based on the departmental reports. This ambitious project has led to recommendations for change in the general studies program, including dropping some courses from the program.

As part of the general studies course assessment, departments were asked to submit course syllabi. A review of the submitted materials made it clear to the general studies subcommittee that some departments needed to do a better job of helping students understand that general studies courses are part of an overall program rather than a series of isolated courses. The committee is soliciting new master syllabi for general studies courses, which will emphasize programmatic goals and the overall coherence of the program.

Discipline-Specific Assessment. In order to obtain information at the discipline level, each of Ball State's seven colleges has adopted its own approach to assessment. Each has prepared an assessment plan that provides a framework for assessment in the college. It describes the college's overall approach and expectations about assessment. It also describes how the college and departments will interact and how assessment results will be used. Each college's plan sets expectations for its departments. For example, the College of Sciences and Humanities has asked each department to create and carry out a separate assessment plan, and Teachers College has asked its departments to report on assessment activities on a five-year cycle.

As a result of these approaches, a wide variety of discipline-specific activities are in place across the university, including portfolios, standardized tests, surveys, focus groups, classroom assessment, and other methods. The activities are chosen by the colleges and departments and carried out by these units, often with support from the Office of Academic Assessment.

In fall 1991, the College of Business faculty began their assessment efforts with an inventory of existing assessment activities and a complete review of the curriculum. This was followed by course-based assessment of the undergraduate core and major. The college's Master of Business Administration (MBA) program was also assessed. The college's approach to core assessment now includes a midcore pre-and postexam as well as assessment of foundation knowledge in the capstone core course. The college's assessment efforts have led to major curriculum revisions, including the introduction of a communications course and the redesign of the production management course. The MBA program has also been redesigned.

The College of Fine Arts relies primarily on portfolios for assessment, whereas the College of Architecture and Planning uses juries. The latter unit has adopted a collegewide approach to many of its assessment activities. For instance, the faculty have developed alumni and employer surveys to follow up on graduates from all departments.

Impact of Assessment. Because Ball State's assessment program has been in place for several years, it is appropriate to ask what the impact of the program has been. It is often difficult to trace the impact of university-wide assessment projects, specifically because of their scope. The information provided from these studies often reinforces information that is being learned from discipline-specific activities in the colleges and departments. In other cases, the results from these studies prompt colleges and schools to collect additional information. For example, the finding from both senior and alumni surveys that about 80 percent of our graduates feel they are very well or satisfactorily prepared with respect to using computers at work has led many individual departments to increase instruction about computers and to develop computer competency assessments for graduates. Although the 80 percent figure may sound high, the university's goal is that all graduates be competent in the use of computers in their disciplines.

Many departments have introduced curriculum changes based on assessment activities. For example, the Department of Telecommunications faculty altered its major requirements to include the study of foreign languages, and the Department of Philosophy increased the amount of writing required from its majors. The Department of Special Education developed a required course addressing legal and procedural issues. Based on results from the Educational Testing Service (ETS) Major Field Achievement Test, faculty in the Department of Biology added a course to the curriculum containing more emphasis on a physiological-organismal approach. Students' scores on the ETS exam improved as a result.

Areas of Strength

A number of factors have contributed to the progress Ball State has made with respect to assessment. Most important has been the leadership that has come from several directions. The view that university-wide assessment activities should be useful to the disciplines has helped foster assessment. It has been important that assessment results have been reported and shared in varied and meaningful ways. An additional factor has been the recognition that if faculty are going to be asked to participate in assessment activities, they should be provided appropriate support in terms of faculty development and reward.

Leadership. Assessment has benefited from the clear vision of the university president and from the solid commitment of both the provost and associate provost to see that assessment is widespread across the university. The director of general education, now also dean of University College, has shepherded a long and arduous five-year cycle of assessment of general education courses. He has been supported in these efforts by the general education subcommittee of the university senate. Individuals on this committee have devoted countless hours to carrying out assessment. Leadership has also been strong in colleges and departments. Fortunately, the benefits of assessment have captured the interest and imagination of many individual faculty, who have made important contributions and are firmly committed to assessment. Faculty in the Department of Philosophy have been very creative in selecting and using assessment techniques, including the Watson Glaser Critical Thinking Appraisal, the Defining Issues Test, and writing portfolios. Faculty members in the Department of Mathematical Sciences developed a holistic scoring rubric for a pre-and posttest for its majors. Several assessment projects developed by Ball State faculty have been featured in a recent book containing assessment case studies (Banta, Lund, Black, and Oblander, 1996).

Integrating University-Wide Assessment with Discipline-Specific Assessment. Undertaking successful assessment remains a challenge, particularly at large, comprehensive universities where colleges are often viewed as quite independent of one another. In designing its assessment program, Ball State intended for the university-wide assessment activities to be conducted and integrated with discipline-specific assessment activities. This has been accomplished in a number of ways.

First, each university-wide project is managed by a committee of representatives from across the university. Generally, at least one faculty member from each college will serve on the committee. This helps ensure that the concerns of each of the disciplines will be represented in planning, and it creates a vehicle for the dissemination of results. Further, it provides an important avenue for the collaboration that is so important to assessment.

Second, for many university-wide projects, we have been able to create separate reports for each college and department, illustrating the responses of its own majors. This is possible because students who participate in our assessment projects are assured of confidentiality, but they are not anonymous. The questionnaires that are mailed to students contain labels including their names. This means that, except for the few who remove the labels, respondents are identified. Identification of respondents facilitates follow-up mailings. It also allows us to obtain demographic information from the student database, including the major area of study. This allows us to create separate reports based on students' majors.

The reports that are generated for colleges and departments frequently follow a particular theme. For example, one report focuses on results that have to do with career issues; another focuses on computer competency results. These reports contain departmental-level tables with college and university comparative figures. Each college can then compare its results with university averages.

Another successful strategy has been to allow colleges and departments to prepare supplements for university-wide surveys. Nine supplements were prepared for the most recent alumni survey. These supplements were mailed with the main survey to the relevant alumni. This approach allows the colleges and departments to prepare questions that are of particular concern to them. By providing coordination, the university helps avoid the situation in which alumni are asked the same or very similar questions by more than one office.

As with discipline-specific assessment, assessment of general studies is also supported by university-wide activities. For example, the senior survey asks seniors to rate their preparation in a number of areas drawn from the goals of the general studies program.

Reporting Results. The Office of Academic Assessment has developed a series of strategies to report results. Each major assessment activity is described in a written report that includes the purpose of the activity and the findings of the project. These reports begin with a comparison of the respondents with the group of eligible students. This information is important in establishing how representative the study group is with respect to the population. The reports also contain information comparing recent results with studies conducted in previous years and with results from related studies. For example, the senior survey report contains a section contrasting results from seniors with results from alumni. Another section contrasts the importance that seniors and freshmen place on various life goals. Although these reports take a considerable amount of staff time to develop, they provide a very thorough accounting of the project and have been invaluable as current and historical reference materials.

In order to provide an overview of assessment projects, a summary report of assessment findings from several projects is updated annually. These reports contain a brief description of each project along with important project findings. They are sent to senior administrators, deans, and department chairs. Department chairs circulate the reports to their faculty.

A series of "Assessment Notes," which includes six or seven major findings about a topic, is also distributed directly to individual faculty members. More recently, a flyer of results organized by theme and titled "Expressions" was sent to all faculty and professional staff, as well as to university donors. The title was chosen because the results of many of our assessment activities reflect our students' collective voices. The themes included on the flyer were acquiring knowledge, continuing to learn, expressing satisfaction, and gaining experience. Extracts of studies often appear in university publications and sometimes appear in local and regional news coverage. In addition to written reports, project results are shared through presentations and discussions. When practical, controversial results are shared individually with interested parties in advance of written reports.

Faculty Development and Rewards. Although there are many faculty who enthusiastically embrace assessment, there are some who are not familiar with what assessment is or confuse it with faculty evaluation. Others have an informed view of assessment, but are reluctant to participate. Ball State's major assessment efforts have been greatly facilitated by various kinds of faculty development initiatives. The Office of Academic Assessment conducts workshops to help departments plan, design, and carry out assessment activities. Several workshops were held in conjunction with the general studies course assessment. Because faculty from each department were developing their own instruments, it was important to provide them with assistance. The initial workshops were designed to engage faculty actively and contained several exercises for them to complete. It quickly became apparent that these materials could be combined into a workbook. In fall 1992, an *Assessment Workbook* was created and shared with the faculty (Palomba and Associates, 1992). This workbook, organized around assessment techniques, has been very well received. Each chapter contains a question-and-answer section as well as checklists and exercises. The Office of Academic Assessment has shared this workbook with many faculty both inside and outside the university.

In addition to workshops conducted by the Office of Academic Assessment, presentations have been organized by several colleges and departments around assessment themes. For example, the School of Nursing held an assessment workshop about portfolio assessment.

Recently, the Office of Academic Assessment has created a series of working groups to introduce classroom assessment to the campus. The group of twenty-five faculty meet once a week for six weeks to study, design, and implement classroom assessment techniques. Each participant is provided a copy of the classroom assessment handbook authored by Angelo and Cross (1993). They also receive a $200 stipend for trying classroom assessment techniques in their classrooms and reporting back to the working group about their results.

In addition to providing staff and material support, the Office of Academic Assessment awards summer assessment grants to faculty who are designing and carrying out assessment activities. Grants are awarded based on several criteria. The most important consideration is how well the proposed activities will move assessment forward in the particular college, school, or department.

A key question is how the information generated by the project will be used. For several years, the office conducted a competitive grant process. More recently, summer projects have been generated through a development process whereby the deans and department chairs identify assessment needs within the department. Using this approach, it is possible to address the most pressing assessment issues in the department. Faculty are then invited to participate in projects. This has led to a greater number of team rather than individual projects. At the conclusion of the project, faculty are asked to submit a brief report describing the project itself, as well as how and when the results will be used. Thoughts and ideas for future assessment projects are also requested. The amount of the grant is generally between $600 to $1,200 per individual, depending on the number of faculty involved in the project. These grants, although small, serve to recognize the contributions that faculty members are making to assessment.

The summer grant program has been very successful. A real attempt has been made to distribute funds as broadly as possible. As a result, nearly every department and college and more than 150 faculty have participated in the program during the past several years. Much of the assessment activity that is currently occurring on campus was initially generated through the grant program. The summer grant program has been described in a recent book about assessment practices (Banta, Lund, Black, and Oblander, 1996).

With so many departments and colleges involved in assessment, a growing number of faculty are being asked to present their results at national conferences. Faculty from the School of Physical Education have presented their assessment plan at national meetings and have had an excellent response. Limited travel funds to support these presentations are available through the Office of Academic Assessment. Funds have been made available to faculty from mathematics, business education, physical education, and other departments. Colleges and departments also provide support for this travel. All of these faculty development efforts, including workshops, materials, grants, and travel money, have been very successful in encouraging faculty participation in assessment.

Continuing Challenges

Although assessment is widespread at Ball State, there are several overriding issues that continually need to be addressed. These issues include involving faculty in assessment, motivating students to participate in assessment, and using assessment results to create change. Ball State has addressed these issues in a variety of ways.

Involving Faculty. It is very important that faculty be involved in assessment and, even with efforts at faculty development and reward, this continues to be a challenge. The university's seven colleges have approached this in different ways. For example, the College of Business expanded the responsibilities of its existing curriculum committee to include assessment. In contrast, the College of Sciences and Humanities created a separate assessment committee.

Although the Office of Academic Assessment has had a faculty advisory committee for several years, the university senate has just created a faculty committee that will replace the office advisory committee. The responsibilities of the senate committee are to identify assessment issues, to disseminate information about assessment, and to recommend appropriate policies for assessment. The committee's work will not impinge on curriculum control or evaluation of individual faculty. The new committee will be made up of faculty elected through the senate process. This should increase the visibility of assessment in the senate.

Another factor that will help foster assessment in the coming years is the increasing interest and involvement of professional accreditation groups. The colleges and departments that have the greatest continuing interest in assessment are often those that have accreditation standards that are specific to the discipline. The College of Business, which is accredited by the American Assembly of Collegiate Schools of Business, has been an assessment leader at Ball State. Other disciplines that have made great strides with assessment programs are speech communication, nursing, and teacher education. All of these areas have professional bodies that have fostered assessment.

Involving Students. Involving students in assessment presents a continuing challenge. Students need to know the purposes of assessment. During orientation, Ball State provides a flyer for entering students and their parents that describes the assessment activities in which freshmen are expected to participate. In addition, a statement about assessment is contained in the university's undergraduate catalogue in a section addressing university values. The statement notes the role of assessment in enabling the university to improve its educational offerings, and it indicates that students are expected to participate in assessment activities.

Students also need to receive results from the assessment activities in which they participate. Our entering freshman survey (MAP) results in individualized reports for students, which are available a day or two after they take the survey. However, the standardized testing that is done in orientation provides group rather than individual results.

The Office of Academic Assessment has used incentives to increase student participation. In addition to cash prizes, the university offers free books for one semester as incentives. Two or three prize winners are randomly chosen from all of the students who participate in selected survey projects.

Occasionally, assessment activities have been modified to increase student involvement. For example, the MAP survey was administered on computer disks for several years. This required students to go to computer labs to take the survey. At times, labs were already reserved for other purposes and the students could not take MAP. Although more than 50 percent of the class took MAP on computers, we have now made MAP available on scan sheets as well.

Students were also very vocal about the writing competency examination. They thought this exam duplicated assessment in their writing courses. It has taken a steady stream of messages to help them see the relevance of the test. Initially, the essay topics were very general and were made available to students before the exam. The test procedures were recently modified so that students sign up for test sessions, where they receive essay topics related to their majors. The topics are now made available at the test sessions rather than in advance. These procedures have increased student motivation with respect to the exam.

Using Results. The most challenging job for assessment practitioners is to ensure that assessment results will be used. Programmatic assessment involves taking collective results from individual students and asking what these results imply about the program itself. Although faculty are quite comfortable assessing individual students, it is sometimes difficult for them to decide how to go about programmatic assessment. At Ball State, the departments are expected to look at assessment results and ask what they imply about academic programs. Individual departments must wrestle with these issues when they develop and carry out department assessment plans.

Some of the most important decisions about usage were made at initial planning stages, such as who will review results and who will make recommendations. For example, the currently existing curriculum committee became the "home" for assessment results in the College of Business. The College of Sciences and Humanities has required that all requests for programmatic change be accompanied by assessment information.

Facing Other Challenges. Assessment does not take place in a vacuum. Other pressures at the university often take precedence. Ball State has experienced some decline in its freshman-year retention rate and in overall enrollment. At the same time, there has been an internal attempt to reallocate funds into salaries. These pressures can divert attention away from assessment, because it is difficult to ask faculty to do more when there are fewer resources available. Throughout this period, the administrative commitment to assessment has been unwavering. Assessment has not been treated as an activity that is optional, but one that is expected and continuing.

Looking Ahead

With support from several areas of the university, assessment should continue to make an important contribution at Ball State.

Role of a Central Office. The development of assessment at Ball State has been greatly shaped by the existence of a central office. This allows for an administrative structure that has continuity and that can focus exclusively on assessment issues. The staff of the office have been available as a resource for assessment efforts throughout the campus. They have also been available to develop assessment materials. Thus, they have been able both to conduct the university-wide assessment projects that originate in the office and to support the general education and discipline-specific projects that originate elsewhere. The very existence of the office makes a clear statement about the commitment of the university to assessment. However, with a central office there is always the risk that assessment will be seen as "something the administration does." The office at Ball State has tried to combat this view by encouraging and supporting assessment in the disciplines and by trying to make the results of university-wide assessment projects widely available and useful to the colleges and departments. Overall, the existence and support of the central office provide focus and continuity for assessment.

It is important to note what the Office of Academic Assessment does not do. It does not require any departments or colleges to report the results of its assessment activities to the office. Reporting requirements for departments are determined in the colleges. Departments also participate in periodic reviews to the Commission for Higher Education. Likewise, the results of the mandated general studies course assessment were provided to the appropriate senate committee, not to the assessment office. Because the office does not have any mandated reporting requirements, the office staff are viewed as facilitators and consultants rather than monitors of assessment.

Other Support for Assessment. Ball State's experiences demonstrate clearly that assessment must be supported by the university. In addition to the support that comes from the Office of Academic Assessment, continuing support comes from many other sources. The Office of Institutional Research, University College, the writing competency program, student affairs, and the university computing services all have expertise that has been drawn on. In addition, many individual faculty members have been more than happy to share their knowledge and experience with faculty outside their own departments.

Next Steps. In the future, the Office of Academic Assessment will continue to play the support role it has played. The office is exploring new ways of making the data that are collected available and meaningful to the university community. The office is currently proceeding with plans to put assessment information and results on a World Wide Web page and is also exploring survey administration via the Web. The general studies committee of the university senate is currently making plans to begin the second five-year cycle of assessment. The second cycle will be organized in a manner similar to the first. Faculty from the newly created College of Information, Communication, and Media are developing a college plan for assessment. The College of Architecture and Planning has undertaken a national benchmark study of assessment outcomes in its disciplines. The College of Sciences and Humanities is encouraging its departments to increase the use of direct measures of assessment through capstone experiences. This information will add to the existing use of indirect measures such as surveys and interviews. Many promising assessment projects are proceeding throughout the campus. There has also been, and will continue to be, a willingness to review and modify assessment procedures so that they provide the most meaningful information.

Summing Up. Ball State has been involved with assessment for several years. Although the beginning of the process was clearly marked by the creation of a central office, the overall university community was allowed to accept the value of assessment gradually. At times, there was apathy, if not resistance, and some of this continues. It appears, however, that the potential of assessment to improve the education of our students is now widely understood and valued. An appreciation of the reasons for and benefits from assessment is now embedded in the culture of the university.

The overall commitment of the university to assessment continues to be clear and strong, and university leaders continue to play active roles. From a period of exploration, the university's assessment program has matured into a coherent, multilayered program. A history of assessment information is now available, and current project results are eagerly anticipated. University-wide assessment activities continue to contribute to our understanding of our students and of their experiences, successes, and areas for improvement. Results from university-wide studies are made widely available throughout campus.

In addition to the central office conducting assessment activities, all colleges, departments, and schools now engage in these activities, which are supported by faculty development initiatives. Many colleges and departments have introduced programmatic changes based on assessment results. The general studies course assessment has contributed to an integrated view of the program and its goals. It has made everyone aware of the strong administrative support and institutional commitment to carrying out and assessing our program of general education.

The process of creating and discussing assessment has had positive results. It has helped focus attention on issues of curriculum, and on teaching and learning. With continued involvement of students and faculty, and with an emphasis on programmatic issues, assessment continues to have great potential to improve education at Ball State.

References

Angelo, T. A., and Cross, K. P. *Classroom Assessment Techniques: A Handbook for College Teachers.* (2nd ed.) San Francisco: Jossey-Bass, 1993.

Ball State University. "Academic Assessment Plan." Muncie, Ind.: Ball State University, Fall 1992.

Ball State University. "Academic Assessment in the Colleges and Schools." Muncie, Ind.: Ball State University, Spring 1993.

Banta, T. W., Lund, J. P., Black, K. E., and Oblander, F. W. *Assessment in Practice: Putting Principles to Work on College Campuses.* San Francisco: Jossey-Bass, 1996.

Palomba, C. A., and Associates. *Assessment Workbook.* Muncie, Ind.: Ball State University, 1992.

CATHERINE A. PALOMBA is director, Offices of Institutional Research and Academic Assessment, Ball State University.

This chapter describes Ohio University's transition from curiosity about the institution-wide impact of assessment on students to program- and department-based assessment for improving teaching, learning, and student services.

Ohio University's Multidimensional Institutional Impact and Assessment Plan

A. Michael Williford

This chapter describes an institutional commitment on the part of Ohio University to assess its students that began in 1981 and has grown steadily for over fifteen years. Ohio University's assessment program, the Institutional Impact Project, has evolved from general curiosity about program quality to a commitment to assess its students continually. Although the state of Ohio has never mandated assessment in any form, since 1981 Ohio University has been using student assessment.

In 1981, Ohio University made an institutional commitment to using student assessment information in program review, curriculum planning, and academic program planning. Academic colleges, planning groups, individual departments, and trustees rely on outcomes information for both short-term and long-term planning and decision making. One purpose of student assessment in Ohio University's planning processes is to assist in improving the performance of programs and students. This is accomplished by providing academic units (colleges, schools, and departments) with regular updates on the progress of students and an assessment of their programs.

Through its planning and information systems, Ohio University regularly makes available to its units institutional, college, and departmental data. It has an ongoing system of quality improvement that has become part of its institutional culture. For example, the Office of Institutional Research provides the colleges and departments with data on student demographics, course enrollments, and faculty staffing and productivity to assist them in their program evaluation and planning needs.

The Institutional Impact Project at Ohio University has helped the institution document its progress in enhancing quality over the last decade (Williford and Moden, 1993). Various indicators of quality at different levels of the student experience gauge separate but oftentimes related qualities. These measures help demonstrate changes over time and assist the university in reaching its goal of improving program quality. They provide evaluative information in relation to the university's goals and planning processes.

Ohio University's experience with assessment can be described in two phases. The first phase was devoted to providing university-wide assessment information to faculty and staff. The second phase was devoted to supporting individual academic units in their needs for assessment information.

Phase One: University-Wide Assessment

In the first phase of assessment, Ohio University's ten-year plan (Ping, 1980) stated that the university had a responsibility to define and examine its growth in quality (Williford, 1991; Williford and Moden, 1993). In 1981, a task force of faculty and staff was appointed by the president to spend a year developing, with the assistance of the director of institutional research, a systematic and ongoing program of assessing institutional quality and the impact of instruction on students. The goal of this first phase was to have reliable data within five to ten years to evaluate the progress of individuals and programs in achieving their goals.

Institutional Impact Project. This program addressed university-wide goals from the Ten Year Educational Plan, including "providing our students with the knowledge and skills which are the essence of a solid liberal education" and "encouraging the development of an environment on the residential campus that reflects a vital commitment to learning and provides a community life for students" (Ohio University, 1977, pp. 18, 38). A multidimensional program was proposed and accepted beginning in the fall quarter 1981 to provide a variety of assessment measures at various times—entry, in process, and exit. Ohio University has used its Institutional Impact Project to help implement its mission and to examine and assess its quality to enhance its effectiveness (Williford and Moden, 1993).

The original Institutional Impact Project had five components. The first was the American College Test's College Outcomes Measure Program (ACT COMP) Objective Test. This is a standardized test of general education knowledge and skills. It is used to assess Ohio University's general education program. Second, student tracking, retention, and graduation rate data were used to provide information about retention and graduation characteristics of groups of students. These were used in the university's retention programs. Third, there were five student surveys—three different student satisfaction studies, which assess how students perceive they are treated by faculty and staff, and two student involvement studies, which assess the activities in which students are involved. Fourth, the freshman marketing study is a survey of admitted first-year students, which assesses why students apply for admission to and enroll at Ohio University. Fifth, two follow-up surveys of graduates (conducted one year after graduation and five years after graduation) yield student outcomes information. The outcome information is of interest to administrators concerned with university-wide outcomes, and it is of interest to individual colleges and departments.

Uses of Institution-Wide Assessment Information. The uses of institutional impact assessment data at Ohio University have been well documented (Moden and Williford, 1987, 1988; Nelson and Williford, 1991; Williford, 1990; Williford 1991; Williford and Moden, 1987, 1989, 1996a, 1996b). Overall, university-wide assessment has been used to enhance the quality of programs (Williford and Moden, 1993). In addition, three basic internal applications have been identified. First, assessment information is tied closely to the university's strategic or long-range plans from the 1980s. These plans address institutional quality. Second, assessment information is used in the university's ongoing planning processes. Decision makers use assessment information in developing their programs. Third, assessment information is used in the university's curricular review processes. Curricular reviews use student outcomes assessment information to make judgments about academic programs.

Because most of the institutional impact studies include population (not sample) data, it is possible to report the results broken down by academic college and department. Colleges and departments receive results on their own students and can make departmental and institutional comparisons over time. These data are also used for Ohio University's academic program reviews. Academic program review assessment data are used by academic departments when departments are reviewed every seven years by the university curriculum council.

External use of assessment information has benefited Ohio University (Williford and Moden, 1993). Performance funding for general education and program-specific awards (such as Program Excellence, a part of the Ohio Board of Regents' Selective Excellence program) have been secured because Ohio University has been doing assessment. Assessment has been used to give the university recognition for responding to calls for accountability and for giving attention to examining quality ("OU: Testing, Testing," 1987). Having over ten years of assessment information has enabled Ohio University to respond to statewide reviews of efficiency and program quality.

The most recent external application of Ohio University's assessment information was the result of a statewide mandate that Ohio's public colleges and universities appoint task forces to study how institutions are managed (Williford and Moden, 1993). The Ohio University task force, Managing for the Third Century, was charged with evaluating the productivity and effectiveness of the university. One of the questions task force members asked was: Is Ohio University using resources economically, productively, and effectively? In response, the task force was given assessment information from the Institutional Impact Project, which enabled the members to document growth in quality and productivity over a ten-year period. The task force recommended implementing a university-wide continual quality improvement program that built on the original Institutional Impact Project.

Specific examples of how Ohio University's assessment program has been used to effect program improvement are found in Moden and Williford (1988, 1996) and Williford and Moden (1996a, 1996b). Each study in the Institutional Impact Project has been used according to its own application. For example, follow-up studies of graduates are used to provide timely and relevant information to Ohio University's nine academic colleges for their own planning and decision making. Student affairs staff have used studies of patterns of student involvement to evaluate and improve student development programs. They also have been used extensively in student retention programs, in which individual students are identified as potential leavers and helped with any problems they might have. Studies of student treatment have been used to improve individual student services offices on campus.

Although the original Institutional Impact Project was conceptualized with faculty and staff involvement, its operation is carried out through the efforts of institutional research staff. In the first few years of the implementation of the Institutional Impact Project, most of its surveys grew from sample surveys to population surveys. Although the university's executive administrators and college deans made use of university-wide findings, individual academic units wanted breakdowns of results on their own students. The desire for these breakdowns depended on the units' individual needs and circumstances. For example, specialized accrediting agencies, such as the National Council for the Accreditation of Teacher Education or the American Assembly of Collegiate Schools of Business, in each of which Ohio University is a member, require institutions to collect assessment information. Additional funds were secured from the provost's office to enable the Office of Institutional Research to provide population data to nine academic colleges and sixty academic departments. These breakdowns are provided annually to the colleges and departments.

Phase Two: Department-Based Assessment

The second phase of assessment at Ohio University began with the intervention of the North Central Association (NCA) of Colleges and Schools, Commission on Institutions of Higher Education. In 1989, the NCA acted on the strong belief that student assessment is vital to improving student learning and academic programs by requiring its member institutions to have practical assessment plans (North Central Association of Colleges and Schools, Commission on Institutions of Higher Education, 1996). By 1996, NCA expected institutions to have fully implemented assessment plans.

Evaluating the Institutional Impact Project. In 1993, Ohio University had its ten-year NCA review. The site evaluators collected information on Ohio University from the required self-study and talked to many different faculty and staff during the campus interviews. Ohio University was well known to NCA's peer institutions for its university-wide assessment program. Indeed, in 1983 Ohio University was praised by NCA reviewers for having been a leader in student assessment (Moden and Williford, 1987). Yet, when the 1993 NCA reviewers interviewed faculty, it became apparent that faculty were not involved in student assessment because the institution had not persuaded them of its importance. Faculty who were interviewed either did not know of the Institutional Impact Project's existence, or they assumed that it was an administrative function performed by the Office of Institutional Research and therefore had little direct relevance to their own academic program's specific needs. As a result, NCA required Ohio University to redraft its assessment plan to focus on department-based assessment. NCA provided the needed incentive to persuade faculty to be more involved in student assessment.

Developing Department-Based Assessment Plans. As a result of the NCA review, in 1993–94, the provost asked Ohio University's academic deans to work with their faculty and the Office of Institutional Research to draft department-based assessment plans. Using a program evaluation model, the departments developed learning objectives for their students and methods to assess achievement of those objectives, using both existing assessment methods and new methods. They identified faculty or groups of faculty responsible for assessing the students and a time line for implementation. They articulated possible uses for the assessment information, recognizing uses as the most essential component of the process. As requested by the president and provost, the stated goal of each department's assessment plan is to improve teaching, learning, and student services. Department-based assessment activities were designed to address major programs of study and service courses, both undergraduate and graduate, on the Athens campus and each of five regional campuses.

Development of the new plan occurred in three phases: identification of current college and departmental uses of Ohio University's centralized assessment, the Institutional Impact Project; identification of current college and departmental assessments already under way; and development of new college and departmental assessment activities. Institutional research staff worked with the colleges to identify their current assessment activities and uses. Resources were made available (sample assessment plans, relevant articles, NCA publications, assessment guides, sample tests, and group and individual consultations with institutional research staff) to assist the colleges and departments in developing their individual plans.

Colleges submitted lists of current assessment activities to the Office of Institutional Research for inclusion in the university's plan. Many of the assessments identified were traditional evaluation activities, such as classroom grading and student evaluations of teaching. The faculty themselves recognized these procedures as inadequate for the new department-based plans. Other assessments were found to be in place, such as professional certification examinations or senior capstone courses, but most of these were not systematically linked to program improvement.

It became apparent that colleges and departments needed to learn more about the purposes of assessment—improving teaching, learning, and student services. Although some colleges and departments viewed developing an assessment plan as a positive opportunity for program improvement, some resentment about developing an assessment plan for NCA surfaced. The administration needed to involve faculty more in the assessment process. Once faculty began to realize the institutional commitment to and the rewards of assessment, they became more involved and committed.

Departments were given one ten-week academic quarter to develop their assessment plans. Institutional research staff provided support and training during this time. Sessions with department chairs and sessions with faculty were held. These meetings were usually explanatory in nature, communicating to faculty what NCA expected, providing examples of previously identified effective assessment activities (from on- and off-campus), and dispelling myths about assessment—its purposes and uses.

Two Types of Assessment. During these activities, it was discovered that assessment at Ohio University could be divided into two distinct types. First, assessment *was* being used for improving student learning. Ohio University's faculty were using a variety of sources of information to assist individual student learning. Some of these sources were organized and systematic, according to individual needs, and some were anecdotal. All that needed to be done with this type of assessment was to organize the data and make its collection and application systematic.

The second discovery was that assessing students for the purpose of improving programs was less prevalent and less well organized. Faculty typically addressed program "improvements" either through adding courses in which needs could be identified or through internal curricular reviews. It was clear that faculty were more comfortable with curricular issues, whereas administrators were discussing program quality. There were problems with terminology between faculty and administrators. Herein lay the greatest challenge in implementing department-based, faculty-involved assessment—to develop a common language about the meaning of and uses for student assessment.

Once the department-based assessment plans were submitted to the Office of Institutional Research for inclusion in the university assessment plan, they were edited and condensed to fit the form of the newly created department-based assessment plan. The new plan was called the Institutional Impact and Assessment Plan, preserving the nature of the original Institutional Impact Project and incorporating the breadth and depth of the department-based assessment plans. The Institutional Impact and Assessment Plan was submitted to NCA in January 1995. The remainder of 1994–95 was devoted to working with and involving faculty to develop a common language for and understanding of assessment and preparing for implementation in 1995–96.

Since the development of the 1995 assessment plan, student assessment has been organized at three levels—institution-wide assessment, institution-wide support of department-based assessment, and department-based assessment. First, the Institutional Impact Project yields institution-wide information about student learning, student outcomes, and services to students. Second, because Ohio University already had a long history of providing the academic colleges and departments with assessment information, the Office of Institutional Research has enhanced its support of department-based assessment. Third, each department is responsible for assessing its own students. This department-based assessment can draw on information from the first two levels, but departments also need to collect their own assessment data.

Implementing Department-Based Assessment Plans. After the plan was completed, the college assessment coordinators and the director of institutional research continued to meet to share ideas about and experiences with assessment. The Institutional Impact Project itself is evaluated annually by this group. Information about the department-based assessment activities is shared among the colleges.

In distributing copies of the complete (two hundred pages plus) assessment plan to all academic departments in March 1995, Ohio University's president announced to the colleges and departments that the university would renew its commitment to assessment and would begin implementing the department-based plans beginning in 1995–96. Further, assessment was put on an annual cycle. In the first cycle, faculty were encouraged to meet throughout the entire year to address and implement their department's assessment plans, paying particular attention to information that the Office of Institutional Research provided. It was also suggested that they begin early to identify what new assessment data they would need to collect. Ultimately, they were encouraged to use new and existing assessment information to determine if they were meeting their department's objectives as specified in their department's plans. Summary reports from each college were due in the provost's office at the end of each spring quarter, beginning in spring 1996. Along with these suggested activities, the colleges and departments received a distribution schedule of institutional impact information (institution-wide, college-specific, and department-specific), so they would know what to expect and when from the Office of Institutional Research.

Departments undertaking new assessment activities incurred new expenses. Accordingly, the provost increased the budget of the Office of Institutional Research to provide modest central financial support for new assessment activities. This support is limited to materials for assessment, such as the Educational Testing Service Major Field Achievement Test or the Graduate Record Examination. Because department-based assessment is viewed as a regular component of faculty responsibilities, support is not available for faculty reimbursement or release time.

A communication strategy was designed that would hold faculty in each department accountable for engaging in assessment. Each department is asked to prepare brief (four to eight pages) reports on its assessment activities and results. These reports are shared among the colleges for comment, review, discussion, and implementation. From the department, a summary goes to the college's dean, who reviews and comments and either returns for revision or forwards to the provost.

Departmental reports are to have four basic components. These components are communicated by answering the following questions: (1) What are your department's goals? Include a brief statement on how they were developed. (2) What evidence do you have of accomplishing your goals? Provide information that documents how the department is accomplishing its goals. Give specific examples. (3) What improvements, enhancements, and developments have been implemented based on the above? (4) What changes do you recommend for your department in the future—in academic program and curriculum—in your department's assessment plan (goals, objectives, methods)?

At the end of spring quarter 1996, departments submitted their first assessment reports to their college deans, who then submitted them to the provost. These reports were brief summaries of how their original plans were implemented and program improvements made or planned.

In 1995–96, a university-wide assessment policy committee of faculty was appointed by the president to discuss implementation and review of department-based student assessment results. In June 1996, the provost, on the advice of this policy committee, appointed another faculty committee to review the assessment reports. The committee recommended resource allocation to specific units for the purpose of improving undergraduate education. A total of $200,000 was set aside for reallocation, and six awards were made in 1996–97.

Awards went to six programs on the basis of their reported assessment activities. These programs had clearly stated objectives, focused on student assessment of processes and outcomes, and documented how they had accomplished or were accomplishing their objectives, especially as a result of assessment activities. A list of best practices in assessment was established from this first year of assessment activity. They are a clear statement of department-specific goals that matches reported assessment activities; faculty involvement in curricular assessment and improvement; use of multiple measures for assessment data; use of information already gathered and distributed by institutional research; integration of departmental, college, and university missions; a focus on student outcomes with emphasis on both benchmarks and value-added measures; improvements based on results or a plan of how results will be used for improvement; assessment activities or other elements of the model that are generalizable to other units; and a continuum of assessment activities from first year to work experiences.

Implementation of department-based student assessment at the university-wide level of review also will be accomplished through the curricular review process. This process was redesigned in 1995–96 by the university curriculum council review committee. Instead of asking departments to provide documentation on the strength of their curricular and faculty resources, the new review process asks departments to provide evidence that they have improved the quality of their programs—teaching and learning—using student assessment information.

Future Directions for Assessment

Ohio University's achievements in student assessment have been facilitated by many factors. Early interest by the president initiated the program in 1981. Faculty and staff in the institutional impact task force recognized a need for this type of information as Ohio University attempted to enhance its program quality. Support and resources from the provost's office were provided. Institutional research staff maintained the components of the Institutional Impact Project, making information available for academic colleges and departments. Curricular reviews increasingly relied on assessment information in evaluating program quality. Specialized and regional accreditation organizations provided external motivation to continue and expand assessment activities. Also, a new president in 1994 and a new provost in 1996 brought renewed interest in assessment to Ohio University.

Obstacles. Two basic obstacles have blocked Ohio University's progress in assessment. The first is a lack of common language between administrators and faculty. Many of the assessment activities carried out by departments are traditional evaluation activities, such as classroom grading and student evaluations of teaching. In other departments, some more effective outcomes assessment activities are in place, such as professional certification examinations or senior capstone courses, but they are not systematically linked to program improvement. Administrators and faculty need to continue to engage in dialogue about the purpose of assessment—improving teaching, learning, and student services.

The second obstacle relates to the potential uses of assessment. The initial motivation for doing department-based assessment was extrinsic. NCA provided an external need for departments to do assessment, but this need was not intrinsic to departments' goals. The need for assessment locally was displaced by the belief that assessment information was to be used externally. A misunderstanding existed that agencies such as NCA were reviewing individual departments, rather than encouraging departments to review themselves with student assessment information. The administration has responded by providing opportunities for discussion about assessment—through personal visits and meetings—so that faculty are beginning to realize the intrinsic benefits of assessment. In addition, the administration has repeatedly communicated that assessment is a movement toward program improvement that will not go away, only to be replaced by the next educational fad. As a result, faculty have begun to realize that there is value in Ohio University's embracing assessment for internal program improvement. Yet, it continues to be important to communicate why assessment is valuable and what the benefits are for faculty at the department level.

Need for Flexibility in Responding to Change. The Institutional Impact and Assessment Plan that was created in 1994–95 is a flexible strategy that specifies objectives, assessment activities, and uses of outcome data. It recognizes that changes in objectives, activities, and uses will develop over time. Indeed, departments are encouraged to review and revise their objectives in the very first cycle of assessment reporting.

Other changes, internal and external, will influence assessment at Ohio University. Internally, the president and provost share a renewed commitment to assessment and are seeking input from the faculty about how to link assessment to planning and resource allocation. The university curriculum council has recognized that curricular review should be based on student assessment to demonstrate program quality.

Ohio University is acting on the president's assessment policy committee's recommendations. The committee recommended that all academic units be involved in assessment, including interdisciplinary programs. The committee recommended bringing assessment experts to campus and sending faculty to assessment conferences. The committee also recommended institutional review of departmental assessment activities and linking resource allocation to those activities.

Externally, the state of Ohio does not currently mandate assessment in any form. However, two recent initiatives in Ohio are linking resources to performance measures, and some of these measures are assessment-based. The first initiative is limited to Ohio's forty-five two-year technical colleges, community colleges, and university branch campuses (Ohio University has five branch campuses). Nine service expectations were identified by the Ohio Board of Regents (OBOR). These expectations were transformed into performance measures. Two-year campuses submit annual reports to OBOR to compete for incentive funding. Ohio's thirteen public universities are subject to a similar initiative. Performance funding appears to be gaining interest in Ohio. Ohio University's assessment program may be influenced in the future by the pursuit of such funding from the state.

The purpose of assessment at Ohio University is to assist the institution's units in enhancing program quality. A current goal is for faculty to become more involved in assessment so that they will know more about and become more involved in their programs and with their students. A future goal is for students to become more involved in assessment so that they will know more about themselves and become more involved in their education.

Although the primary purpose of assessment nationally is to enhance teaching and learning, the principles of assessment can be used to address other missions—research and scholarly activity and public service. Though assessment is a tool for Ohio University to refocus its publicly perceived primary mission of instruction, the president and provost have suggested that the other missions should be included as well. Future goals for assessment may be to address issues of quality in creative and scholarly activity and service to the community. Assessment provides a framework for institutions to address quality of a full range of programs—teaching and learning, research, and service.

References

Moden, G. O., and Williford, A. M. "A Multidimensional Approach to Student Outcomes Assessment." Paper presented at the Twenty-Seventh Annual Association for Institutional Research Forum, Kansas City, Mo., May 1987.

Moden, G. O., and Williford, A. M. "Applying Alumni Research to Decision-Making." In G. Melchiori (ed.), *Alumni Research: Methods and Applications for Institutional Enhancement*. New Directions for Institutional Research, no. 60. San Francisco: Jossey-Bass, 1988.

Moden, G. O., and Williford, A. M. "Applying Alumni Assessment Research to Academic Decision-Making." In T. W. Banta, J. P. Lund, K. E. Black, and F. W. Oblander, *Assessment in Practice: Putting Principles to Work on College Campuses*. San Francisco: Jossey-Bass, 1996.

Nelson, P. E., and Williford, A. M. "A Ten Year Study of Communication Graduates." Paper presented at the World Communication Association Conference, Jyvaskyla and Helsinki, Finland, May 1991.

North Central Association of Colleges and Schools, Commission on Institutions of Higher Education. "Commission Statement on Assessment of Student Academic Achievement." *North Central Association–Commission on Institutions of Higher Education Briefing*, July 1996, *14* (2), 6.

Ohio University. *Ohio University Educational Plan: 1977–1987*. Athens: Office of the President, Ohio University, 1977.

"OU: Testing, Testing." *Columbus Dispatch*, Apr. 10, 1987, p. 14A.

Ping, C. J. *Quality Dependent on the Making of Judgments*. Athens: Office of the President, Ohio University, 1980.

Williford, A. M. "Using Student Involvement in Value-Added Outcomes Assessment." Paper presented at the Thirtieth Annual Association for Institutional Research Forum, Louisville, Ky., May 1990.

Williford, A. M. "Ohio University's Multidimensional Assessment Program." *Assessment Update*, 1991, *3*, 14–15.

Williford, A. M., and Moden, G. O. "The Use of Alumni Outcomes in a Multidimensional Institutional Impact Assessment Program." Paper presented at the Twenty-Seventh Annual Association for Institutional Research Forum, Kansas City, Mo., May 1987.

Williford, A. M., and Moden, G. O. "Using Alumni Outcomes Research in Academic Planning." Paper presented at the Twenty-Ninth Annual Association for Institutional Research Forum, Baltimore, Md., May 1989.

Williford, A. M., and Moden, G. O. "Assessment and Quality Enhancement at Ohio University." In T. W. Banta and Associates, *Making a Difference: Outcomes of a Decade of Assessment in Higher Education*. San Francisco: Jossey-Bass, 1993.

Williford, A. M., and Moden, G. O. "Assessing Student Involvement." In T. W. Banta, J. P. Lund, K. E. Black, and F. W. Oblander, *Assessment in Practice: Putting Principles to Work on College Campuses*. San Francisco: Jossey-Bass, 1996a.

Williford, A. M., and Moden, G. O. "Assessment of Student Treatment." In T. W. Banta, J. P. Lund, K. E. Black, and F. W. Oblander, *Assessment in Practice: Putting Principles to Work on College Campuses*. San Francisco: Jossey-Bass, 1996b.

A. MICHAEL WILLIFORD is director of institutional research and assistant professor, School of Applied Behavioral Sciences and Educational Leadership, Ohio University.

Eventually, assessment must tell us more about what is going on teacher by teacher, course by course. Do we have the commitment to find out?

Assessment of General Learning: State University of New York College at Fredonia

James R. Hurtgen

Initial Activities

The College at Fredonia is a comprehensive undergraduate college of the State University of New York (SUNY), with an enrollment of 4,500 students. Fredonia is located fifty miles southwest of Buffalo near the southern shore of Lake Erie. In 1980, Fredonia's faculty governance body instructed its academic affairs committee to prepare a set of recommendations for revision of the college's general education requirement. This initiative was strongly urged, and strongly supported, by the vice president for academic affairs. Following three years of campuswide discussion and planning, the college instituted a new general education requirement in 1983.

Prior to its revision, Fredonia had a thirty-six credit-hour distribution, the general college program (GCP), which was required of all students. It was the common view of the faculty that the GCP lacked a clearly articulated set of learning goals. The goals that one might discern in the program were not consistently addressed in the courses available. There was inadequate attention to writing. All students were required to take the standard one-semester English composition course. Beyond this, there was no other specified writing requirement (though clearly some GCP courses involved a substantial amount of formal writing by students). The program paid no attention to issues of cognitive or cumulative skills development as students moved through it. Though certainly many sound, well-taught courses were available to students, there was truly no program to the program. Neither was there any systematic faculty oversight of the GCP. Fredonia's GCP was simply a bunch of courses.

The revised GCP remains a thirty-six credit-hour requirement but is now divided into three parts. In Part I, four different courses focus on the development of writing, reading, computational skills, and analytical thinking. Part II consists of six courses taken outside the major. These courses introduce the natural sciences and mathematics, the humanities, and the social sciences. Part III involves two required upper-division courses outside the major, which are designed to integrate learning from Parts I and II. Courses in each part are meant to build on the skills of the preceding parts. The position of dean for liberal and continuing education (later retitled dean for liberal studies) was created to manage the revised program and to chair the newly established faculty committee responsible for developing the learning guidelines for each part of the program as well as for reviewing and approving all courses submitted for inclusion in the program. As with the previous program, the revised GCP would depend on courses supplied by each of the college's departments. However, the new GCP had three things the previous program lacked—an explicit set of learning objectives tied to each of its parts, a faculty oversight committee, and a dean.

After consensus was reached on the goals and the design of the revised program, the logical next step was to assess whether the program was meeting its professed learning goals. Thus, at the inception of the program, Fredonia's faculty governance body mandated that learning outcomes of the new GCP be assessed. The new dean and the assessment committee that she convened decided that assessment of the new program would be rigorous, requiring that an effort would be made to assess student learning directly in the skills identified as the central goals of the GCP. In 1986, the college sought and received a three-year grant from the Fund for the Improvement of Postsecondary Education (FIPSE) to plan and administer an assessment of general learning specifically tied to the learning goals built into the design of the GCP. The assessment project was firmly supported by our president and vice president for academic affairs. Specifically, a yearly assessment budget was provided to supplement FIPSE funds. These funds assisted in the professional development of GCP assessment committee members, most of whom had no particular background in learning theory or measurement. Travel to workshops and conferences was supported. Assessment practitioners were brought to campus to work with the assessment committee as well as with other groups of faculty. The dean and the vice president were energetic in keeping the entire faculty informed about the work of the assessment committee. This not only helped sustain awareness of what was happening but also sent a clear message to the campus that this project was a high priority of the college administration.

During this period, two additional developments aided the effort to assess general learning at Fredonia. First, Fredonia's president instituted a system of assessment-based planning shortly after his arrival in 1985. Hereafter, resource decisions would be guided by assessment outcomes along with the standard inputs (student demand, program requirements, curricular innovations, and the like). Second, following discussions between the SUNY provost and the university's faculty senate, a SUNY-wide assessment initiative was announced. Campuses were instructed to prepare comprehensive assessment plans. The plans would be campus-based. SUNY would not dictate the means, but it did insist on the preparation and implementation of plans that would assess majors and general education at each campus. In short, Fredonia's General Education Assessment Project anticipated campuswide and university-wide initiatives that helped sustain it through what turned into a ten-year effort.

The FIPSE Assessment Project

As FIPSE project director, the dean for liberal studies convened the committee of twelve faculty members to design and score a set of tests intended to determine the learning outcomes for students following completion of the GCP. The committee rejected the use of any of the growing number of standardized tests created by national testing services on the ground that they were not designed to measure the specific outcomes that Fredonia's GCP was intended to foster.

After much study and discussion, the committee developed nine "paper-and-pencil" tests to assess student mastery of the following skills: writing, reading, quantitative problem solving, scientific reasoning (two tests), reflexive reasoning and socioethical reasoning (three tests). Testing began in the fall of 1988. Each test was given to a sample of forty first-year students and forty juniors and seniors who had completed the relevant parts of the GCP. Both freshman and upper-class samples were matched for high school average. Mean grade point averages and the standard deviation from the mean for all groups approximated those of the entering freshman cohort. To determine the effect of various competing factors, including maturation (and the effect of the GCP) on student learning, samples of freshmen and upper-division students were tested at Miami University. Two-person faculty teams independently scored each test without knowledge of the class level or school of the test takers.

Findings. Findings were reported to the campus in August 1989. A second administration of the tests was started in 1991. Groups of students were tested as entering freshmen. The same students were given the same tests as juniors at the opening of the spring 1994 term. A second report of findings was distributed to the campus in the fall of 1995. The first report (1989) to the faculty noted that most of the mean scores for Fredonia upper-division students were higher than those for Fredonia freshmen. Upper-division students' scores were significantly higher than freshmen scores in writing, reading, and socioethical reasoning. Although score differences were not uniformly significant for each of the subtests of reading and socioethical reasoning, the improvement shown by upper-division students in writing was uniformly significant for each of the writing subtests. However, upper-division students did not score significantly higher in scientific reasoning, quantitative problem solving, or reflexive reasoning. They showed the least apparent progress in the critical thinking skills identified in the test of reflexive reasoning. Leaving aside the question of score improvement or its lack over time, it must also be said that the absolute scores of freshmen and upper-level students were frequently low. Interestingly, freshmen tested at Miami University in general scored at about the level of Fredonia upper-division students, though the differences in scores between Fredonia freshmen and upper-division students were greater than those for Miami freshmen and upper-division students. This led the assessment committee to conclude cautiously that Fredonia's "different trend might suggest that our courses, and the ways we teach them, are having an effect on our students that exceeds the effect of maturation alone" (Amiran, 1989, p. 6).

Following analysis of the scores for the second administration of the tests, the 1995 report to the faculty highlighted once again that there was general improvement in the learning levels of our students as they moved through the curriculum. However, this time the weaknesses that students demonstrated in the area of reflexive or critical thinking as compared with the other skills tested were even stronger than in 1989. As in 1989, the upper-division students demonstrated significantly more advanced improvement in their socioethical reasoning skills. Upper-division students scored significant gains in quantitative problem solving and in their understanding of the elements of scientific reasoning (though once again scores of both freshmen and juniors remained low). The 1995 report notes *no* significant gain in the students' demonstrated writing or reading ability—two areas that showed significant gain in the late 1980s, especially writing.

In summary, after taking our tests twice over a six-year period, students showed consistent strength in socioethical reasoning (particularly in the awareness of their own values) and consistent weakness in reflexive reasoning, that is, the ability to reflect systematically on their own thinking. Disappointingly, the significantly higher scores noted in writing and reading among upper-division students in 1989 were not repeated in 1995. On the other hand, the weaknesses seen in scientific reasoning and quantitative problem solving in 1989 did not appear again in 1995. Thus, except for social scientific thinking (consistent improvement) and reflexive thinking (consistent nonimprovement), student performance appears to be variable in the skills our GCP is intended to strengthen.

Curricular Changes Following First and Second Testing. One of the changes resulting from the revision of our general college program was to increase the upper-division courses students would take outside their majors. In practice, this resulted in students taking more upper-division courses in the social sciences, particularly in history, anthropology, and political science. Because many of these courses require lower-division prerequisites, the present GCP has induced an increased exposure among students to courses that emphasize the abilities associated with our tests of socioethical reasoning. In fact, one of the curricular consequences of the revised general college program is that many students take a substantial portion of their electives from courses approved for the GCP. It is not uncommon for a student to complete more than

60 of 120 required credit hours in courses that fulfill the GCP. Moreover, in the spring semester of 1991, we held a six-day workshop (three days in January, three in May) for faculty on ways to increase the cross-cultural and international foci of their courses. Although the workshop was not restricted to faculty from the social sciences, most faculty who involved themselves for both the January and May sessions were from these disciplines, with a small number from the humanities. Participating faculty developed specific changes in their courses that formed the basis for discussion and debate during the workshop sessions. In view of the increased number of credit hours our students take in the social science disciplines resulting from changes in our general college program, it is reassuring to note that the skills associated with socioethical thinking are the only ones that showed significant improvement from freshman to junior year on each occasion that these skills were assessed.

The need to encourage improvement in student writing was a major reason for revising our general education requirements in the early 1980s. Like faculties and administrations of so many institutions around the country, the faculty and administration of Fredonia moved to spread writing throughout its curriculum. We cannot say by how much the amount of formal writing increased, but we believe it did increase, based on changes in course-taking patterns among students and changes in individual course requirements. (Trying to systematically measure this increase proved maddeningly difficult.) The traditional one-semester course in English composition was bolstered by a second writing-intensive course, which students can take in their own majors—and many do.

Because increased attention to the writing process was now the responsibility of all faculty, not just those from our English and foreign language departments, the college instituted a series of writing workshops for faculty. Workshops were led by an experienced, highly respected member of our English department and given to groups of five to six faculty from different departments. Faculty participants for each workshop were carefully chosen to ensure that exchange between them would be free and mutually respectful. The participants sharpened their understanding of how to use and evaluate student writing in their courses by doing a good deal of their own writing and critiquing in the workshops. Faculty were paid generous stipends to participate.

By the summer of 1995 when the last workshop was offered, close to one hundred—about 40 percent—of our faculty, representing all our academic departments, had taken one of the workshops. Why, then, did significant writing improvement not continue from one test administration to the next? We do not know. Among the possible answers are these: although the sample of students whose writing was retested in 1994 was representative of students as a whole in their college grades and majors, they may not have been representative in the mix of courses they had taken through five semesters of study. Or, the students who completed the test in 1988 may have been stronger writers than our students as a whole. Perhaps the results of each test administration are representative, but we have begun to lose energy for the commitment to improving student writing. It must be noted also that our test of writing required students to prepare an essay during a fifty-minute period. Few students will ever be given a formal writing assignment in college that must be completed in fifty minutes. Thus, there is a question about the validity of the test of writing.

Following the initial report of findings to the faculty in 1989, two study groups were convened to recommend ways that faculty might help students overcome perceived weaknesses in their ability to identify biases and assumptions in what they read and think and in their problem-solving skills. One year later, these groups issued reports with sample exercises tied to specific courses (that is, courses given by the study group members). The reports were made available to every member of the faculty. There was no formal follow-up to determine what use the faculty made of these reports. It is clear though, through informal observation, that some of the faculty employed these reports in their teaching, at least for a time.

A single faculty development workshop on ways to improve the teaching of problem solving in two GCP mathematics courses was given in the summer of 1990, but not repeated. What happened? Upper-division students achieved significantly higher scores in one of the two versions of the test of quantitative problem solving as reported in 1995. However, whereas a good deal of attention was given to ways to improve student writing and socioethical understanding, with what seems like mixed success, no particular initiatives (aside from changes made by individual faculty) were taken following the first assessment to improve learning in the natural sciences. Nonetheless, students registered significant gains in 1995 in their understanding of scientific method.

The Departments of English and History recently instituted a portfolio requirement for their majors. Students are required to include a number of formal papers in their portfolios over the course of several semesters. Each paper is submitted with a page or two of critical comment by the students about their work. These papers and accompanying commentary are discussed periodically by the students and their faculty advisers. Papers may be submitted from courses in several departments. We could not determine the effect of the portfolio requirement at the time of the second GCP assessment because of the newness of the requirement and because too few students from any one department were represented among test takers.

In the spring of 1995, the college's faculty council created an ad hoc committee to examine the implications of the GCP assessment findings and to recommend revisions to the structure and goals of the program as it deemed appropriate. In the spring of 1996, this committee reported a preliminary proposal in which it recommended, first, that all departments be required to offer one or more writing-intensive courses sufficient to meet the GCP requirement for each of their majors. Though several of our departments now offer approved writing-intensive courses, there is no college requirement that they do so. Heretofore, recommendations from the administration to mandate at least one writing-intensive GCP course in each department were resisted by faculty governance committees (and several departments). The second assessment report helped change minds on the issue. Second, the committee recommended that increased attention be given to cross-cultural and international issues in lower-division GCP requirements. This requirement is formally included only in the upper-division requirement of six credit hours. Third, as a means to increase the intellectual coherence of the GCP, the committee recommended that courses in different parts of the program be clustered by common subject or thematic focus. This recommendation does not bear directly on the findings from the assessment project. However, we hope that this change, if implemented, will increase interest among students in the GCP and therefore their commitment to its goals.

Finally, encouraged by the GCP assessment results as well as by assessment in our majors, the dean of the faculty sponsored three continuing faculty workshops starting in the spring of 1996 to address new pedagogies in the teaching of writing, in supplemental instruction, and in the application of instructional technologies in the classroom.

What Worked and What Didn't

Fredonia's General College Program Assessment Project confirmed two things: first, that a group of dedicated college faculty can design and implement an ambitious set of tests to assess general learning based on the particular design and goals of the curriculum; second, that it is enormously difficult in practice to administer these tests over time in ways that meet rigorous canons of validity and reliability. The work of the initial faculty committee of twelve members from ten of our departments stimulated much careful thought and discussion, not only among themselves but also across the campus. This was a major source of the commitment to the goals of general education that was reflected in the GCP.

As noted, we must be cautious in drawing conclusions from the results of our tests of general skills development at Fredonia. We cannot say definitively that higher scores, when they occur, are attributable to course work specifically associated with the general college program. Because the combination of courses taken by each student on the way to the bachelor's degree is so varied, we can probably never get further than informed, but uncertain, judgments about what the curriculum is doing. It seems reasonable to suppose that faculty development workshops are effective in helping faculty design course requirements and projects that will further the goals of the curriculum (though no workshops were given on how to develop reliable and valid tests). But more important than workshops is the constancy of attention to the goals of a general education program. This is achieved by embedding the goals in as many courses as possible. It is very likely that this is the conclusion to be drawn from our apparent success with socioethical reasoning. It is very common for our students to take no fewer than five social science courses at Fredonia regardless of major.

We have not yet met the goal of spreading writing throughout our curriculum. Or so it seems. As noted, there is a problem with the test of writing itself. Students were required to write an impromptu essay in a fifty-minute period, but this is not the kind of writing we are working to improve. Faculty, who as a group are not prone to overestimating the skills of their students, report judgments of genuine improvement in writing from the freshman to the junior year. They just do not trust the unsatisfactory results of the second administration of the writing test. Aided by word-processing software that makes the correction process simpler (independent of any assistance given by spelling and grammar checkers), students are turning in better work. This is what we think. But increased attention to writing was also supposed to improve student reading and thinking. We do not see any evidence of this. Indeed, changes in the curriculum aimed at helping students improve their reflexive reasoning do not show any apparent positive results yet. The 1995 report shows that students increased their scores significantly between their freshman and junior years in quantitative problem-solving skills and in their understanding of scientific reasoning, both significant gains in their ability to reason. However, the failure to improve in the ability to reason self-critically, or, reflexively, is the cause for greatest concern in the 1989 report and again in the 1995 report. Our students continue to demonstrate a limited inclination to examine, much less test, the assumptions and biases that undergird their thought.

The GCP Assessment Project produced models of tests for use by specific departments. For example, the history department has adapted the tests of socioethical reasoning to assist faculty in assessing learning by history majors. Similar, though necessarily more demanding, tests of scientific reasoning can be administered by our natural and social science departments to their majors.

Subsequent Signs of Progress and Problems

FIPSE support of our GCP Assessment Project was critical both for the funding it supplied and for the visibility it gave to an ambitious effort to assess general learning by the use of a set of homegrown tests. The bulk of the FIPSE funds were used to support the cost of test development by the twelve-person committee over a three-year period. Once the tests and scoring manuals were developed, and FIPSE support ended, we were able to conduct the second administration of the assessment tests at a dramatically reduced *financial* cost. Nonetheless, considerable time and administrative support were needed for the second administration as well as for training the faculty committee and scoring the tests.

We demonstrated that faculty who have no particular background in the kind of testing employed in our project can join those with such a background to design appropriate tests inside and outside their fields. Though the committee included one measurement specialist, it was primarily composed of dedicated amateurs, who brought genuine excitement and curiosity to the task.

Faculty of widely varying backgrounds scored the second round of tests. For example, a biologist joined a historian in scoring the tests of socioethical reasoning. A philosopher and a psychologist scored the test of scientific reasoning.

Our experience with assessment brought to light a number of problems. When the results of assessment are in, what then? Of course, the answer seems obvious. You focus your energies on improving instruction and learning in those skills that require strengthening, and work to maintain student competence in the areas in which they are already strong. But how? Knowledge about an area of student weakness, for example, in the elements of effective writing, does not itself impart much insight into the pedagogical strategies that might help students overcome weaknesses in writing. One way in which we have stumbled at times is by failing to distinguish diagnosis from prescription in talking about our response to assessment.

Second, planning for assessment must be accompanied by planning for the response to its findings. We cannot know the outcome of assessment in advance, but one can expect the need for some changes in curriculum and instruction. The mechanism for stimulating these changes should be discussed along with assessment and carefully planned as the second part of the two-step process of improving undergraduate teaching and learning. We did not give sufficient attention in our plans to the ways in which we would systematically use the results of assessment.

A third problem concerns what might be called the "ownership issue." Fredonia's current general college program is truly an improvement over its predecessor, but its predecessor is familiar to fewer and fewer faculty who continue to teach at the college. Similarly, the ambitious and thoughtful project that was begun ten years ago to assess general learning at Fredonia is loved best by the faculty who spent countless hours and great intellectual effort to design it. To a person, this group of faculty reported that their own teaching was energized by the work they did in familiarizing themselves with the challenges posed by rigorous assessment. Inspired by their reading and discussions, they made changes in their teaching before the results of assessment were available. Reading between the lines, one is led to conclude that these faculty benefited more from designing the tools for assessing general learning at Fredonia than the college did from administering these tools.

This suggests that different groups of faculty should take responsibility for the assessment of general learning over time. This is indeed what we did in undertaking the second administration of the FIPSE tests. (Necessity dictated this in part; four of the original committee members were no longer on the faculty.) Among the eight faculty members who made up the team to score tests for the second assessment, only one was a holdover from the first administration. However, in extending the sense of ownership in assessment by increasing the number of faculty involved in it, we also increased concerns for the reliability of test scores. So we face a dilemma. Confine scoring to the same group of faculty over a period of several years (assuming that the same faculty are available) and minimize a test reliability problem. Or, involve different faculty (out of necessity or prudence) and confront a reliability problem even as you increase the sense of ownership in assessment among the faculty.

A fourth problem is this: if every course is assessed, none is assessed. We designed Fredonia's assessment of general learning to be non-course specific. This makes sense. No single course (not even English composition) is intended to bear individually the challenge of helping students master the skills built into the GCP. By design, these skills are to be met by widely varying combinations of courses. Because this is so, individual faculty members have no way of determining whether the courses they offered for the GCP contributed to the scores in student learning that emerged from the assessment project. In the absence of comparable outcome measures based on the work of their own students, faculty members cannot know what impact their own teaching is having on learning. This quite possibly works to distance the faculty from the results of global assessment projects. Accordingly, assessment on the scale of Fredonia's tests of general learning cannot replace assessment on a smaller scale, that is, assessment within a major or other discrete set of courses.

It should also be noted that because we could not control for the effect on student skills development resulting from course work outside the GCP, we were unable to assess outcomes demonstrably resulting from courses taken as part of the GCP. This does not mean that the results are any less valuable, only that it is not a specifiable part of our curriculum that was being assessed. What began as an effort to evaluate part of the curriculum ended as an assessment of virtually all of it.

A fifth problem concerns what general learning assessment told us about teaching—which was less than we would like. As noted, Fredonia's students demonstrated gains and losses in different skills when assessed in 1989 and 1995. For example, in 1989, juniors did not score significantly higher in scientific reasoning than the freshmen test takers. However, students tested in the second administration increased their scores significantly between their freshman and junior (or senior) years. Does this mean that instruction in the courses that focus on scientific reasoning has improved? Not necessarily. Improvement may have been the result of better instruction by the particular mix of faculty from whom the thirty-five to forty tested students took their courses. Those who took courses from a different mix of faculty might have achieved no significant score gains. Based only on the different results of the two assessment projects, we do not know whether teaching has improved in some skills, like scientific reasoning, or deteriorated in others, like writing, because there was no way to control for the different mixes of faculty whose teaching was presumably being assessed, at least indirectly.

What did we learn, then, about direct assessment of general skills learning at Fredonia? One important lesson we learned is that rigorous testing on the scale that we attempted it is fraught with a host of difficulties. To mention but one: we can design serious tests, but we cannot guarantee that students will take them seriously. Despite these difficulties, assessment of general learning at Fredonia yielded something of great value. It helped us refocus our minds on the important questions: What do our students need to learn? Are we helping them learn it? Do we know, or can we learn, better ways to get the job done? The GCP Assessment Project did not give us answers to these questions that can stand up to rigorous scientific scrutiny. But it did give us a basis for informed judgment, and this is surely valuable enough.

A number of factors are at work that will help us sustain the assessment of learning at Fredonia. Every academic department is required to prepare and implement assessment plans on a five-year cycle. Some departments have adapted our GCP assessment tests to their own programs. A bimonthly assessment newsletter is distributed campuswide. This newsletter summarizes assessment activities of departments and individual faculty. The newsletter is a forum for good ideas, and, as such, has served to encourage faculty to try something new. The committee that produces this newsletter is a standing subcommittee of the college's planning and budget committee. The latter reports directly to the president. In short, assessment of student learning and development is now a part of the process by which we make fundamental decisions about the directions of the college.

Looking Ahead

We do not expect general learning at Fredonia to be reassessed in the next five years. Our energies will be devoted to redesigning our general college program and to assessment in the major. It seems that it is more important for us now to assess pedagogies than the design of our general education curriculum. This is where we end up in any case. A curriculum or major is a construct. Students do not complete majors, not literally. They take courses from individual faculty members. Their courses are grouped, yes. But learning results from the interaction of the student with the teacher and the material, course by course. The next step must be, we think, to learn more about what is going on teacher by teacher, course by course.

Reference

Amiran, M. R. *The GCP and Student Learning: A Report to the Faculty.* Fredonia: State University of New York College at Fredonia, 1989.

JAMES R. HURTGEN is on the faculty of the political science department, State University of New York College at Fredonia. He was formerly dean for liberal studies.

This chapter analyzes the effect of an evolving organizational culture on a community college's effort to build and sustain an institutional effectiveness program.

An Extended Journey to Assist At-Risk Students

R. Dan Walleri, Juliette M. Stoering

Beginning in the late 1970s, budget constraints and accountability concerns led to a reassessment of the mission of community colleges and their effectiveness. These issues were later articulated in influential writings, such as Parnell's *Neglected Majority* (1985) and the Roueche, Baker, and Roueche 1987 article on the "open door or revolving door." Demonstrating that community colleges were truly meeting the needs of at-risk students required the development of sound assessment practices (Ewell, 1983; Kreider and Walleri, 1988).

Origin of Assessment Efforts: Early 1980s

The development of Mt. Hood Community College's (MHCC) assessment program was influenced by national, state, and local factors. At the federal level, the Carl Perkins Act placed particular emphasis on assisting at-risk students in the funding of vocational programs (Searcy, 1980). The evaluation requirement under the Perkins Act was a significant factor in the decision of the deans of students of the thirteen Oregon community colleges to form a consortium and initiate a project focused on the problems of at-risk students in 1979. In addition, the late 1970s was a period of retrenchment in higher education. This condition put a premium on demonstrating effectiveness before state legislatures. In the case of MHCC, national and state factors interacted with local conditions to bring about an institutional focus on assessment of student outcomes and on institutional effectiveness. For the first time since its founding in 1966, MHCC was experiencing significant enrollment declines as well as a decline in both state and local funding. Thus, the focus on at-risk students, and especially the retention of these students, was motivated by both enlightened self-interest and a genuine desire to improve institutional effectiveness.

In 1980–81, a student success task force was formed, under the leadership of the vice president, with a charge from the president to review all institutional policies affecting student progress and to make recommendations for improvements that might increase the prospects for student success (Japely, Kennedy, and Walleri, 1987).

Initial Activities: 1983–1992

In response to the presidential charge to find ways to promote student success, activities were initiated to identify underprepared students and to address their needs. Efforts also were made to assess student persistence in terms of their intentions and goals in attending the college. These activities were later integrated into a broader institutional effectiveness program.

Guided Studies Program and Student Intentions. An analysis of transcripts of at-risk students revealed that some students were spending an extended period of time in developmental education without making any significant progress. Other students were enrolling in college-level course work despite basic skills deficiencies identified in placement tests. At-risk students had very high attrition, and those who were retained generally exhibited poor academic performance. As a consequence, a mandatory testing and placement system for entering students was initiated (Japely, Kennedy, and Walleri, 1987; Walleri, 1996). A guided studies program was implemented for underprepared students to ensure that they did not enroll in college-level courses until deficiencies were addressed. In addition, time limits were placed on students in developmental education, unless the student was making satisfactory progress, and formal exit requirements were put in place.

A student intent information system was established to enable faculty to analyze and understand student persistence. This system allows faculty and staff to track and assess progress based on a student's initial or subsequently defined goals, such as to secure a job, to transfer to a four-year institution, to upgrade job skills, or to engage in personal enrichment (Walleri, 1990).

From Student Success to Institutional Effectiveness. Beginning in the mid-1980s, an effort was initiated by the college president to translate the focus on student success into an institutional effectiveness program. The idea was to build an integrated systems approach to organizational effectiveness (Gray, 1993; Gratton and Walleri, 1993). The first important element in this approach was the assessment of student success in relation to student intentions. This element was then integrated with an instructional program improvement process based on the relationship between student outcomes (retention, job placement, transfer success) and institutional cost. The results of the program review provided input to the third element, strategic planning and resource allocation. The fourth element was staff and organizational development to assist the faculty and staff in better serving students and encouraging continual improvement.

What Worked and What Didn't

The initial activities produced modest improvement in the success of at-risk students. In terms of implementing an institutional effectiveness program, the initial activities were important first steps in achieving information-based decision making and in gaining faculty and staff participation in the process. Nevertheless, the success of these efforts was limited in scope.

Successes and Limitations of Student Success Initiative. The guided studies program touched about 40 percent of entering degree-seeking students. Subsequent cohort tracking showed that the persistence rate and the level of academic performance of at-risk students equaled that of entering students whose placement tests indicated readiness to pursue college-level course work. However, this initiative did not expand beyond the guided studies program. There was no general increase in student success, especially as measured by retention rates. Fewer than 50 percent of entering degree-seeking students are retained through two years, and even fewer achieve a significant record of academic accomplishment as measured by earned credits.

Despite awareness of other strategies, such as an early warning system and an automated degree audit, that could enhance student success, MHCC managers and faculty did not pursue initiatives beyond the guided studies program. One obstacle was ongoing budgetary constraints. A second reason was a generally held perception that the causes of attrition were beyond the control or influence of the college (financial problems, conflict with work schedule, and so forth). This belief undoubtedly influenced resource allocation decisions.

Successes and Limitations of Program Improvement Process. The program improvement process produced comparative information on student outcomes, program effectiveness, and costs, which proved useful to the administration and board of education. As a result, the decision-making process became more information based rather than being dependent on intuition and anecdotal material.

The process did not succeed fully due to the fact that a majority of the faculty never became confident in the integrity of the process. The limitations of the measures and data were part of the problem. In addition, the faculty were not willing to accept balancing student outcomes against institutional costs for a program—that is, most of the faculty simply did not believe that the cost per full-time equivalent enrollment (FTE) was a relevant factor in evaluating programs. Another issue was inequity, the failure to have a counterpart review process for the college and instructional support areas.

Successes and Limitations of Strategic Planning and Resource Allocation. The major value of the strategic-planning process was the high degree of faculty and staff participation. Each budget unit had a plan with identified needs. Cross-campus communication was significantly enhanced by the dissemination of area goals and strategies. The process helped identify areas of duplication and encouraged more collaboration. For example, several of the instructional units were independently initiating classroom research efforts to enhance student involvement. Through the planning process and with the assistance of the staff and organizational development department, faculty from the different areas were able to collaborate and thus enhance their projects. However, the process failed to identify institutional direction and priorities. The strategic plan was a compilation of area goals and resource requirements, totaling several million dollars more than any realistic expectation for funding from the college's budget. As a result, it was very difficult to make a logical connection between the strategic plan and subsequent resource allocation decisions.

Systemic Problems

Despite the many efforts aimed at improving student success and institutional effectiveness, the efficacy of these efforts probably was limited and inhibited by problems that are systemic to the institution. General institution-wide support for emphasizing student success and service to the community is undermined by the perception of staff that they are already working toward these goals on their own. Although individuals and their units often make extra efforts to assist students and other campus visitors and constantly look for ways to improve the services they provide, the various units of the campus are unable or unwilling to work collectively (Ewell, 1996). The apparent lack of effective cross-unit communication was first identified in the 1987 accreditation review and continues to be an issue at the college.

The lack of communication throughout the organization provides a partial explanation for why student attrition has continued to be a concern at MHCC. Retention rates in the general student population have remained lower than desired and have shown little or no improvement from one cohort year to the next. Although various units provide excellent service to students and make changes to improve their services, the implementation of such changes and their potential benefits to students have not been effectively communicated to the greater college community. The result has been a variety of piecemeal efforts that lack the campuswide collaboration and support that is needed to make a coordinated impact on student success.

Better communication is also needed among top-level administrators and unit managers, and among the academic and nonacademic units. In particular, meaningful two-way communication needs to take place to clarify both the specific needs of various units and the reasons behind administrative decisions regarding resource allocations in terms of strategic priorities and assessment results.

Subsequent Signs of Progress and Problems: 1993–Present

Demands for accountability have intensified. External demands include efforts such as Oregon's Shared Information System (SIS), which requires all state workforce development agencies, including the community colleges, to report on their performance in moving students to self-sufficiency. SIS is a unit record data system, which allows for matching students' community college records by social security number to statewide reports on employment and wages and reports on the success of community college students transferring to the state's four-year colleges and universities. The SIS provides a means of examining the relationships among students' community college experiences, their employment and wage history, and their success in four-year institutions. As a result of property tax–limitation measures approved by the voters, the state now directly provides the vast majority of funding for education. The governor and legislature will be using the SIS results in allocating scarce funds among the various state agencies.

Another external demand is the recently adopted emphasis on student outcomes by the Northwest Association of Schools and Colleges for the accreditation process. Whereas most of the regional accrediting groups have ten or more years of experience in student outcomes assessment guidelines, the first explicit effort by the Northwest Association did not take place until the 1994 accreditation handbook.

Internal demands have also increased because a statewide property tax limitation has necessitated budget cuts. More than ever before, it has become paramount to base resource allocation on reliable data that guide sound planning.

Factors Facilitating Progress to Date. Through the 1980s and into the early 1990s, the driving force behind development of the institutional effectiveness program had been a single individual. He moved from vice president to president in 1985. After this move, the vice president position was left vacant. Although the various systems that had been previously set up were sustained, it became increasingly difficult for the president to address identified weaknesses because of competing demands on his time and organizational inertia. The lack of any leadership replacement in the area of assessment, combined with budget constraints, limited efforts to maintain existing systems and the status quo. In 1992, the vice president position was filled, and the new person became a catalyst for change that allowed the institution to achieve the following improvements:

Reform of the strategic-planning process. In response to an appraisal of the limitations of the initial strategic-planning process, the college's planning council, including the new vice president, conducted a review and recommended changes. Recommendations included simplifying the process and incorporating Total Quality Management (TQM) techniques into strategic planning. A faculty member with expertise in TQM was granted release time to assist the council in designing a new planning system. These changes led to the identification of specific institutional goals. Every year, these goals are reassessed and prioritized. Each unit or division of the college revisits its area strategic plan on an annual basis and must clearly link its plan to the institutional goals.

Development of program-function review process. One of the institutional goals calls for the allocation of resources based on a program-function review process in accordance with priorities derived from the college strategic plan.

The task force charged with developing the process included staff from a broad cross section of areas on campus, including faculty, in the hope of promoting campuswide cooperation with and confidence in the process. Program-function review is more equitable than its predecessor in that all instructional programs and administrative and student support areas participate in the review.

The process is ongoing and consists of two phases. The first is based on a standard set of indicators that are primarily quantitative. Phase two complements phase one by requiring individualized and qualitative assessment, which includes satisfaction surveys (administered to students and other college staff) and external peer review. The overall review is ongoing and integrated with other related activities such as the accreditation self-study.

Title III grant support for at-risk students. A five-year Title III grant has provided an opportunity to build on previous student success initiatives and it emphasizes assessment. The result is that a comprehensive review of both student services and instruction is under way. The assessment efforts include implementing a new orientation program for entering students, replacing a paper-and-pencil placement test with a computerized adaptive test, conducting curriculum reviews, developing linked courses, and proposing an integrated studies program, to name a few. The heart of these efforts is an intensive intervention program for at-risk students. Counselors and instructors, acting as student advisers, make multiple contacts with individual students each term. The expectation is that retention and success can be improved by demonstrating an interest in a student's well-being and progress.

Assessment matrix. An assessment matrix and activity calendar have been developed in response to the perceived flurry of assessment activities on campus (Walleri and Stoering, 1996). The intention in developing these tools was threefold—to illustrate the integration and overlap of the assessment activities; to promote communication and understanding of them; and by doing so, to foster participation in them.

Role of information technology. An information technology project has provided additional support for the above initiatives. A campus network system has improved communication and facilitated group work. A new management information system will allow for greater access and improved information, especially in the area of student tracking.

Teaching and learning center. The professional and organizational development component has been strengthened through a private grant that has allowed the college to establish a teaching and learning center (TLC). The TLC provides a setting for formal professional development activities, such as training in the instructional uses of computer technology, and it is a place where faculty can informally share and explore issues of concern. For example, the TLC is currently sponsoring a review of the student evaluation of instruction system.

Problems Blocking Progress to Date. Although recent activities have overcome many of the limitations of earlier initiatives, there are still issues that need to be addressed. First, staff cooperation with and participation in the activities need to be maintained. Faculty commitment to the intensive intervention with at-risk students is especially important to cultivate. Second, a stronger system for linking budget development directly to program-function review data and area strategic plans needs to be put in place. As it now stands, program-function review data are used primarily to affirm that programs-areas are doing well, and in some cases, to make improvements. More needs to be done to follow through with difficult decisions about resource allocation based on the review process and to make clear to campus constituencies the explanations for the decisions. Finally, improvements to the student tracking system would facilitate assessment efforts. More accurate, specific reports and a faster turnaround time aligned with the budget development schedule would give the campus more current and reliable information with which to work. This in turn would yield stronger campus support and a stronger tie to resource allocation.

Looking Ahead

Many of the problems that have impeded progress to date may decrease with time because of continued efforts to revise and refine institutional effectiveness at MHCC. The college is also experiencing large-scale changes in administration and technology and at the same time the pressure of constantly increasing budget constraints, all of which may have an impact on student success and institutional effectiveness efforts.

In 1996, both the dean of instruction and the president retired and the vice president resigned. New leadership was brought to the college. Staff are exercising guarded optimism that the new leadership will yield positive changes for the college, yet at the same time, all are aware that budget constraints continue to increase. Most are adopting a wait-and-see attitude toward the new administration, reserving judgment until more time has passed.

Another major challenge is to use new technologies effectively in supporting the institutional effectiveness program. Again, it is too early to tell how much the new computer network system will facilitate the availability of high-quality information and better dissemination of information, but as the college goes through the many stages of implementation, this continues to look promising.

The college is scheduled for accreditation review in the fall of 1997. Faculty and staff are currently involved in the preparation of the self-study document. The accreditation review will be a major test of the institutional effectiveness program and an opportunity to reflect on the progress of the past ten years.

References

Ewell, P. T. *Information on Student Outcomes: How to Get It and How to Use It.* Boulder, Colo.: National Center for Higher Education Management Systems, 1983.
Ewell, P. T. "Results of a Campus Culture Survey at Mt. Hood Community College." Internal report for the National Center for Higher Education Management Systems, Oct. 1, 1996.

Gratton, M., and Walleri, R. D. "An Integrated Systems Approach in Support of Institutional Effectiveness: The Roles of Staff and Organizational Development and Institutional Research." *Staff, Program, & Organizational Development*, 1993, *11* (1), 35–47.

Gray, P. J. "Campus Profiles: Mt. Hood Community College." *Assessment Update*, 1993, *5* (3), 10–11.

Japely, S. M., Kennedy, M. J., and Walleri, R. D. "Assisting Success Through an Improved Student Information System." *College and University*, 1987, *62* (2), 117–125.

Kreider, P. E., and Walleri, R. D. "Seizing the Agenda: Institutional Effectiveness and Student Outcomes for Community Colleges." *Community College Review*, 1988, *16* (2), 44–50.

Parnell, D. *The Neglected Majority*. Washington, D.C.: Community College Press, 1985.

Roueche, J., Baker, G., and Roueche, S. "Open Door or Revolving Door." *Community, Technical, and Junior College Journal*, 1987, *57* (1), 22–26.

Searcy, J. A. *A Project to Improve Vocational Guidance Services and Programs for the High Risk Students in Oregon Community Colleges*. Salem: Oregon Department of Education, 1980.

Walleri, R. D. "Tracking and Follow-Up for Community College Students: Institutional and Statewide Initiatives." *Community/Junior College Quarterly of Research and Practice*, 1990, *14* (1), 21–36.

Walleri, R. D. "A Ten-Year Effort to Assist Underprepared Students." In T. W. Banta, J. P. Lund, K. E. Black, and F. W. Oblander, *Assessment in Practice: Putting Principles to Work on College Campuses*. San Francisco: Jossey-Bass, 1996.

Walleri, R. D., and Stoering, J. M. "The Assessment Matrix: Communicating Assessment and Accountability Requirements to the Campus Community." *Journal of Applied Research in the Community College*, 1996.

R. DAN WALLERI *is director of research, planning, and computer services at Mt. Hood Community College. He is a past president of the National Council for Research and Planning.*

JULIETTE M. STOERING *is research associate in the Office of Research and Planning at Mt. Hood Community College.*

At this point in the history of outcomes assessment in higher education, we believe we have sufficient experience to relate our own generalizations about successful practice to some solid principles that can guide future work in the field.

Moving Assessment Forward: Enabling Conditions and Stumbling Blocks

Trudy W. Banta

This chapter sums up the new take on outcomes assessment in higher education that has been discussed in this volume. It draws some generalizations from points made in the preceding chapters for the benefit of the assessment practitioners who are our readers. In particular, this chapter is designed to provide a framework for those readers who (like this chapter's author) begin a text by reading the summary chapter to gain an overall perspective and to see what to look for in the earlier chapters.   Drawing generalizations from the work of others in assessment is a responsibility with which I have some experience. In 1992, I wrote a final chapter for *Making a Difference: Outcomes of a Decade of Assessment in Higher Education* (Banta and Associates, 1993). In 1995, I wrote another summary chapter for *Assessment in Practice: Putting Principles to Work on College Campuses* (Banta, Lund, Black, and Oblander, 1996). But those chapters were written at decidedly different times in the history of higher education assessment.

In 1990, when I first began to identify authors for chapters in *Making a Difference,* there were very few institutions with much experience in assessment. The chapters in that edited work were written by pioneers like the administrators and faculty at Alverno College and Northeast Missouri State University (now Truman State University), where assessment was first undertaken in 1970, and by administrators and faculty from institutions in Tennessee, Virginia, New Jersey, and Colorado, where public colleges and universities were carrying out the earliest of the state assessment mandates. In 1990, there were very few "experts" in assessment, so few that those with several years of successful campus assessment experience (many of whom were chapter authors in *Making a Difference*) were well known to assessment scholars.

Five years later, the scene had changed dramatically. All the regional accrediting bodies and three-quarters of the states had taken steps to encourage institutions to engage in assessment, and the annual *Campus Trends* (El-Khawas, 1996) surveys were telling us that virtually all institutions were planning, or were engaged in carrying out, assessment initiatives. In trying to assemble a wide variety of examples of interesting assessment practice for *Assessment in Practice,* we eventually developed a mailing list of some 750 individuals at institutions all over the country. Two hundred of them responded by sending us case outlines, and we eventually drew on material from 165 fully developed cases for the book. These multiple sources of evidence tell us that at least a few individuals on most campuses now have had some experience in outcomes assessment.

What we have not yet determined systematically is how deeply assessment has penetrated. At how many institutions has assessment endured beyond the experimentation and early adoption phases that Peter Gray describes in Chapter One? Where are assessment results being used in shaping decisions about needed changes and reallocation of scarce resources? In short, where is assessment making a difference? And most important for the rest of us: If it has been successful, why is this the case? And if it has failed, what were some of the stumbling blocks that others of us can learn to avoid? This issue of *New Directions for Higher Education* and the conclusions drawn in this chapter are designed to provide a beginning point for addressing these questions.

We can take only the first small steps in suggesting the critical factors associated with success in assessment, or lack thereof, because our generalizations are, of necessity, based on the experiences of a very small set of institutions. Nevertheless, we believe we have sufficient experience at this point in the history of outcomes assessment in higher education to ground our conclusions in some solid principles. In fact, in this chapter the nine *Principles of Good Practice for Assessing Student Learning* (American Association for Higher Education, 1992) are used as an organizing framework. A tenth principle, first enunciated in *Assessment in Practice,* is added. The nine principles were developed by a dozen "practitioner-students of assessment," (p. 1) who were brought together for a series of meetings between 1989 and 1992 by Theodore H. Marchese and Pat Hutchings at the American Association for Higher Education, with support from the Fund for the Improvement of Postsecondary Education. The statements about effective assessment practice developed by this group were drawn from the campus experiences of its members plus those of others whom they had observed during a combined total of several hundred visits to colleges and universities across the country. The tenth principle was drafted by the authors of *Assessment in Practice* on the basis of our attempts to incorporate all the characteristics of successful practice cited by the 165 case writers whose work was described in *Assessment in Practice.*

The ten principles of good practice are as follows:

1. The assessment of student learning begins with educational values.
2. Assessment is most effective when it reflects an understanding of learning as multidimensional, integrated, and revealed in performance over time.
3. Assessment works best when the programs it seeks to improve have clear, explicitly stated purposes.
4. Assessment requires attention to outcomes but also and equally to the experiences that lead to those outcomes.
5. Assessment works best when it is ongoing, not episodic.
6. Assessment fosters wider improvement when representatives from across the educational community are involved.
7. Assessment makes a difference when it begins with issues of use and illuminates questions that people really care about.
8. Assessment is most likely to lead to improvement when it is part of a larger set of conditions that promote change.
9. Through assessment, educators meet responsibilities to students and to the public.
10. Assessment is most effective when undertaken in an environment that is receptive, supportive, and enabling [American Association for Higher Education, 1992, p. 2; Banta, Lund, Black, and Oblander, 1996, p. 62].

Principles Confirmed in Practice

In this section, we will take as our fundamental assumption that these ten principles are important for the successful practice of outcomes assessment in higher education. Material from each of the preceding chapters is cited to illustrate these principles. No attempt has been made, however, to draw material from every chapter to illustrate every principle.

Principle One. *The assessment of student learning begins with educational values.* In Chapter One, Gray recalls Everett Rogers's contention (1968) that the extent to which an innovation is consistent with their existing values and past experiences influences the rate at which people adopt that innovation. Several of the authors herein provide powerful evidence of the importance to its long-term success of connecting assessment to an institution's mission, values, and goals.

At Truman State University (formerly Northeast Missouri State University), where assessment has had its longest run, the authors begin: "Assessment can have a profound transformational impact on an institution . . . [if] such core values as the improvement of student learning through the systematic collection of performance-related data and information . . . become integrated into the institution's culture. Successful assessment is much more than techniques, processes, or even outcomes; it is a cultural issue that affects how a community of scholars defines its work and its responsibilities to its students" (Chapter Two). They go on to describe the vital role of Charles McClain, who decided during his first year as president in 1970 that the university had an obligation to provide students with an education that would enable them to compete successfully in graduate or professional school, or in employment, and that the institution should be able to measure the impact of this education on its students. Over the years, McClain and his chief academic officer, Darrell Krueger, were so able to communicate this vision that faculty began to feel strong collective responsibility for their students' success in attaining their educational goals and for assessment as a means of monitoring that success.

Using institutional data to define and then improve program and institutional quality has been an important goal and thus the driving force behind assessment at Ohio University since 1980. The Ten-Year Educational Plan launched in that year by President Charles Ping sought to provide students with essential knowledge and skills in a supportive residential environment. The assessment program thus included measures of knowledge in general education as well as such measures of the learning environment as student treatment by faculty and staff and student involvement in campus activities.

At Mt. Hood Community College, the most important goal enunciated by its president in 1980 was to increase the prospects for student success in relation to their own goals. Assessment was viewed as an important component in an integrated systems approach to organizational effectiveness.

In 1986, Ball State University renewed its commitment to excellence in undergraduate education by adding to its mission statement the intention to undertake "constant and vigorous self-assessment" (Chapter Three). Subsequently, Ball State became the only public institution to receive funds for an academic assessment program from the Indiana legislature.

Principle Two. *Assessment is most effective when it reflects an understanding of learning as multidimensional, integrated, and revealed in performance over time.* Most of the assessment programs at institutions represented in preceding chapters reflect an understanding that assessment findings acquire additional credibility when they are derived from multiple methods that are sustained over time.

Assessment at Truman State University began with nationally standardized exams in major fields and later in general education. Then, surveys of student and alumni satisfaction were initiated. Now, faculty also use a sophomore writing test, portfolios, interviews, capstone courses, and numerous other locally developed instruments to assess student learning. Finally, comprehensive program reviews were instituted on a five-year cycle. Most of these methods have been used continually for twenty years or more.

To a similar array of measures, Ball State adds a locally developed survey for entering students, which asks them questions about their college and life goals, their adjustment to college, their plans for using their time for both studying and participating in campus activities, their self-assessment of knowledge and skills, and their willingness to seek help. Staff from the academic assessment, academic advising, and housing–residence life offices, as well as from the learning center, developed the survey and thus have a vested interest in using its findings to guide improvement in elements of the student experience across the campus. Ball State's assessment activities have been under way for a decade.

The multifaceted approach to assessing student learning and experiences at Ohio University includes a survey for entering students that asks why they chose the school. Later in the first year, these students are asked how they perceive the treatment they have received from faculty and staff and how involved they are in campus activities. By using student tracking data and retention and graduation rates, Ohio University staff are able to evaluate the effectiveness of their retention efforts. Ohio University has sustained most of its assessment activities since 1981.

For more than ten years, institutional research staff at Mt. Hood have used transcript analysis and student intentions data to study the persistence and performance of specific groups of students. Job placement and success at transfer institutions are monitored for former students and graduates.

Principle Three. *Assessment works best when the programs it seeks to improve have clear, explicitly stated purposes.* Assessment at the State University of New York College at Fredonia was initiated in 1986 to monitor the effectiveness of a general education requirement instituted by faculty governance three years earlier. That requirement had specific goals in three areas—developing the skills of reading, writing, computation, and analytical thinking; introducing natural science, mathematics, humanities, and social science concepts; and integrating learning in these areas in upper-division courses outside the major.

In keeping with its mission as a teaching institution, Ball State uses assessment to evaluate academic programs and enhance student learning. In 1991, the Ball State provost issued a statement urging faculty, administrators, students, alumni, and community representatives to work together on assessment and to use the results to stimulate program improvement. More specifically, the assessment program is to determine "the knowledge and attitudes of students when they enter the university, when they complete the general studies program, and when they finish their majors" (Chapter Three).

Principle Four. *Assessment requires attention to outcomes but also and equally to the experiences that lead to those outcomes.* All faculty who teach give individual students feedback about their performance on assignments and tests, which eventually culminates in a grade for the student's record. Outcomes assessment may use the very same assignments and tests, but it results in a collective view of the data—across students and by multiple faculty—for the purpose of evaluating the success of the curriculum and instructional approaches that the faculty have designed and used. This continual attention to the *processes* of teaching and curriculum construction for the purpose of increasing and enhancing student learning is the defining characteristic of successful outcomes assessment.

At Fredonia, cross-disciplinary groups of faculty undertook in 1986 a collective assessment of students' attainment of such fundamental skills as writing; reading; quantitative problem solving; and scientific, reflexive, and socioethical reasoning. Three-person faculty teams scored each test, which was given to samples of first-year students and juniors and seniors. Analysis of the results of the testing gave faculty some sense of what students had learned as a result of their general education program.

Ohio University faculty and staff employ student tracking and retention and graduation statistics to gather information about the persistence of particular groups of students. This information is used to develop individualized approaches that encourage persistence. University-wide questionnaire data reported by college and department enable individual academic units to identify areas in which their success with students is not as great as it is in other units on campus. Thus, faculty can spot areas of weakness and take actions aimed at improvement. In addition, studies of patterns of involvement in various aspects of student life and the yearly evaluations of student treatment by staff in each unit have provided direction for changes in individual student services offices.

Assessment at Mt. Hood initially was aimed at identifying underprepared students and addressing their needs, with the ultimate aim of increasing student persistence. Through analysis of the transcripts of at-risk students and an effort to determine students' initial educational goals, Mt. Hood faculty and staff began to see the value of mandatory testing and placement at student entry and of continuing individualized advising to help students attain their goals—transfer to a four-year institution, secure a job, upgrade skills, obtain personal enrichment.

Principle Five. *Assessment works best when it is ongoing, not episodic.* All of the institutional examples of assessment cited in this volume were selected because they had a multiyear history. The underlying philosophy for assessment as a tool to inspire continual improvement of programs by faculty and staff was established at Truman State in 1970, at Ohio University and Mt. Hood in 1980, and at Ball State and Fredonia in 1986–1987. Although new methods of implementation have been introduced and approaches have been adjusted as experience has dictated needs for improvement, the basic outline of the assessment initiative and the commitment to its purposes have remained intact at these institutions. Moreover, assessment at each institution consists of a series of linked activities, as described above.

Truman State's assessment program was evaluated by the American Association of State Colleges and Universities in 1984 and subsequently was awarded that organization's G. Theodore Mitau Award for Innovation and Excellence. Due in large part to its conscientiously implemented assessment program, Truman State has been cited frequently in national rankings of colleges and universities as a leader in terms of quality and relative costs. In 1985, the legislature designated Truman State as Missouri's public liberal arts and sciences university.

Four of the five other institutional reports in this volume include references to the evaluation of the campus assessment initiative by the appropriate regional accrediting body. Ohio University's story is noteworthy in this regard.

In 1983, the North Central Association review team praised Ohio University's university-wide assessment program. But in 1993, the reviewers left saying that the faculty did not understand or appreciate outcomes assessment and were not sufficiently involved in its implementation. This development has led to a whole new phase of assessment at Ohio University, one that is focused on assessment of student learning by faculty at the individual department level.

Principle Six. *Assessment fosters wider improvement when representatives from across the educational community are involved.* At Fredonia, the faculty governance body issued the initial call for assessment of the institution's new general education program. Then, faculty from a cross section of disciplines came together to develop its tests of basic skills.

Although not initially as involved in learning outcomes assessment as reviewers from the North Central Association (NCA) of Colleges and Schools thought they should be, faculty in all departments at Ohio University are now joining their colleagues in student affairs and the university administration in using assessment for program improvement.

The assessment programs at Truman State, Ball State, and Mt. Hood have been multidisciplinary since their inception, involving faculty and academic and student affairs professionals.

Principle Seven. *Assessment makes a difference when it begins with issues of use and illuminates questions that people really care about.* Assessment at each of the five institutions represented herein has been designed to provide evidence in areas that are deemed important to campus decision makers.

At Truman State, McClain asked if students were being prepared to be competitive nationally in terms of their knowledge and skills. Thus, nationally standardized exams played a major role in outcomes assessment in its early years at Truman State.

At Ohio University, outcomes assessment was designed initially to document and improve institutional quality as defined by the institution's strategic plan. At the outset, the Office of Institutional Research played a pivotal role in assessment by developing and administering a variety of surveys to determine progress of students and graduates in meeting institutional goals. More recently, assessment of student learning by faculty has become another important component of Ohio University's assessment program.

Ball State's assessment program was designed to emphasize and strengthen that institution's role as a "premier teaching university" (Chapter Three). Thus, student learning in general education and the major, satisfaction of students and graduates with their educational experiences, and graduates' success in employment and further education have been the targets of assessment activity.

At Fredonia, faculty instituted a new general education requirement in 1983 and then expressed interests in monitoring its effectiveness by issuing a call for assessment of student learning outcomes associated with the program.

Mt. Hood administrators initially set their sites on assessing student success in relation to stated student intentions. Later, instructional improvement became a goal of that assessment program. Transcript analysis, student tracking, and follow-up of graduates subsequently were chosen as the appropriate assessment measures.

Principle Eight. *Assessment is most likely to lead to improvement when it is part of a larger set of conditions that promote change.* Given each institution's purposes for assessment as outlined in Principle Seven, some evidence of progress can be cited in connection with each institution's approach. In addition, some outcomes of assessment cut across multiple institutions.

Bringing faculty together for developmental experiences was mentioned by virtually all of the chapter authors. Writing across the curriculum was the target for faculty development at Truman State and at Fredonia. At Truman State over the years, 20 percent of the faculty have participated as portfolio readers or as readers for the university-wide sophomore writing assessment. This experience has been influential in creating a common understanding among faculty of both the strengths and the weaknesses of the general education curriculum at Truman State.

With the exception of Fredonia, all the institutions represented here have used assessment data in charting progress toward campus planning goals. Through assessment most have also developed indicators of effectiveness, which they can use in annual reports to trustees, state agencies, and other stakeholders. Truman State, Ball State, and Ohio University collect campuswide data that are then disaggregated by college or department, as appropriate, for use in suggesting unit improvements. All institutions except Fredonia also report using assessment data in comprehensive program reviews.

At Mt. Hood, the assessment-related improvement strategies have brought the performance of at-risk students up to the level of entering students in terms of college-level skills. The faculty-developed general education assessment tests at Fredonia have begun to serve as models for use by specific departments; for example, the tests of scientific reasoning are now given to natural and social science students in courses in their majors. At Ball State and Truman State, several departments have introduced new courses and new requirements on the basis of the data they have collected about student achievement; for instance, the amount of writing required of students in certain majors has been increased.

Principle Nine. *Through assessment, educators meet responsibilities to students and to the public.* Virtually all of the institutions reporting in this volume use assessment findings routinely to report to external stakeholders progress in meeting their stated goals. However, none have been as successful in obtaining external support through their emphases on assessment as have Truman State and Ohio University.

Truman State first used assessment data in 1979 as evidence of the need for specific improvements in four disciplines—language and literature, science, mathematics, and business. The State of Missouri awarded the institution $400,000 for the proposed initiatives. In the mid-1980s, Truman State again used assessment data to show how much student satisfaction with its library had declined, and the legislature responded with funding for library renovation and expansion. Eventually, its emphasis on the use of data to support claims of strength as well as weakness became a factor in Truman State's designation as Missouri's liberal arts and sciences university.

Ohio University's assessment information has been very helpful in responding to statewide reviews of efficiency and program quality in higher education over the last fifteen years. Ohio University's diligence in collecting evidence of program needs and quality has also been rewarded with specific grants from the state for general education and program excellence.

Principle Ten. *Assessment is most effective when undertaken in an environment that is receptive, supportive, and enabling* (Banta, Lund, Black, and Oblander, 1996). There are a few very practical features of the climate for success in assessment that may be implied in the nine foregoing principles but seem worthy of additional emphasis in this tenth standard. These features include administrative leadership, resources for implementation, an atmosphere of trust, and avenues for communicating results.

Administrative Leadership. The experiences of Fredonia, with its faculty-led general education assessment initiative, and Ohio University, with the North Central Association's review, which led to a second phase of efforts to involve faculty in a well-established central assessment program, demonstrate the importance of faculty ownership of assessment. Yet, most studies of assessment also point to the need for strong support from central administrators.

The authors of the Truman State, Ohio University, Ball State, and Mt. Hood chapters cite strong presidential leadership as a compelling force behind assessment at their institutions. At Truman State, then president McClain knew the data and used it in speeches as well as in informal conversations with faculty. How could faculty ignore assessment when their president kept asking them questions about it?

Presidents with an appreciation of the importance of assessment usually appoint a capable person to lead faculty initiatives and to assemble the data that can be collected most efficiently by a central office. At Truman State, this individual was the academic vice president, Darrell Krueger. At Ohio University, Michael Williford in the Office of Institutional Research has taken the lead in assessment, as has Catherine Palomba at Ball State and Dan Walleri at Mt. Hood. The longevity and comparative success of the programs at these institutions are due in no small part to the consistent leadership these individuals have given over the years and to the support they have received from their presidents.

Resources for Implementation. This truth is undeniable: assessment takes some extra time as people must learn to use assessment methods and tools, and time costs money. Assessment tools also utilize resources. Local exams must be devised; standardized tests must be purchased; tests and surveys must be administered. Institutional teams need to attend regional and national assessment conferences. Faculty development workshops must be held on campus.

At Ball State, faculty may apply for summer assessment grants of $600 to $1,200 to develop assessment strategies in their disciplines. More than 150 faculty, representing nearly every department and college at Ball State, have participated in the grant program to date.

At Ohio University, $200,000 was reallocated in 1996 for the purpose of encouraging departments to use assessment data. Awards were made to six programs that had stated clear student process or outcome objectives, had collected data, and had documented improvement actions based on assessment findings. From these reports, a faculty committee derived a statement of best practices in assessment.

Atmosphere of Trust. In addition to providing advocacy and material support for assessment, campus leaders can communicate that assessment will be used for improvement, and will not be used punitively. Magruder, McManis, and Young have conveyed this concept well: "By deliberately fostering a collegial, low-risk environment, McClain and Krueger were able to persuade faculty that they were sincere in their efforts to create an improved university and that faculty had nothing to fear from the assessment system. The trust that was developed between the faculty and the administration provided the necessary support for the enterprise. Because the leadership implemented assessment slowly and because they continually reassured faculty that the data would not be used punitively, they were successful in establishing the environment necessary for their emphasis on improving student learning to be embraced campuswide" (Chapter Two).

Avenues for Communicating Results. Assessment data must be packaged in ways that communicate meaning to the audiences that need to see them. Comprehensive reports are needed for campuswide decision makers, whereas short summaries are appropriate for small groups with a particular, well-defined interest. Comparative data from other institutions or from the same institution at previous points in time should be included. Catherine Palomba has identified some other characteristics of good assessment reports in Chapter Three.

The consequences of failing to communicate widely the purposes, findings, and uses of assessment can be seen in the outcomes of the 1993 NCA review at Ohio University, when recommendations were made to educate faculty about assessment and to involve them in assessing student learning. Walleri and Stoering have included a discussion of communication problems in Chapter Six.

Barriers to Success

The preceding chapters provide lessons not only on successful approaches to implementing assessment but also on barriers to successful implementation.

Lack of Faculty Support. Two recent national studies (Ewell, 1996; Steele, 1996) have identified lack of faculty support as the most significant barrier to successful implementation of outcomes assessment. As Gray suggests in Chapter One, persuading faculty of the importance of outcomes assessment can be difficult initially because they may not understand immediately the differences between individual assessment for purposes of assigning a grade and group assessment for purposes of obtaining information to guide program improvement. Assessment appears to be yet another item in a long list of new responsibilities that faculty are being asked to assume without additional compensation or recognition. Moreover, few faculty believe that time and money spent on evaluation of their work constitute as productive a use of those resources as simply doing more of that work or trying to improve on their own. These are hard arguments to overcome.

The successful developers of assessment at Truman State remind us that not only is it hard to involve faculty initially but it also will remain a problem that is never fully solved, because each year there is a new group of colleagues who need to be convinced of assessment's value. Nevertheless, the presidents at Truman State have managed to win over faculty colleagues.

The chapters by Catherine Palomba and Michael Williford provide excellent suggestions for encouraging faculty to take on assessment for improvement purposes.

Changes in Institutional Leadership. Changes in leadership may make it difficult to sustain assessment. In the late 1980s, Kean College of New Jersey and the University of Tennessee at Knoxville were widely recognized for their pioneering work in assessment. But the departure of key leaders in these institutions resulted in a diminution of the emphasis accorded assessment on those campuses. Truman State appears to be fortunate in that the transition from McClain and Krueger to its current leadership has not diminished the use of assessment data in decision making as a distinctive feature of the institution.

Changes in Institutional Circumstances. Changes in an institution's circumstances can also cause a disruption in the focus on assessment. The authors of the chapters on Ball State, Mt. Hood, and Fredonia discuss the impact of budget cuts on assessment. Activities like evaluation, which are not sufficiently valued, may be early casualties in this environment. Fortunately, there are some institutional leaders, like those at Ball State, who understand that in a crisis, one needs evaluative data more than ever to ensure informed decision making.

Limitations of Assessment Tools and Methods. Serious limitations plague assessment tools and methods. No instrument is perfectly reliable or valid, and most are seriously flawed as measures of the fullness of the concepts we value. Nevertheless, the inability to measure a skill, performance, or trait should never be used as an excuse not to attempt to foster these qualities in students; nor should we give up on a given assessment method because it is imperfect. We must use the measures we have and improve them continually. And we must use multiple measures and pay attention to the common findings they yield.

The seasoned assessment team at Truman State points to the particular difficulty of ensuring that there is acceptable inter-reader agreement among the faculty who grade portfolios in different years. If this measure of reliability is not established, it will not be possible to compare student performance in one year with that in other years. The faculty at Truman State work hard to achieve a high level of agreement among readers.

According to Walleri and Stoering, many of the faculty at Mt. Hood are still not confident in the integrity of the data provided by assessment. This is due in large part to the apparent limitations of the assessment measures that have been used.

Insufficient Involvement of Students. Insufficient involvement of students in assessment can certainly contribute to its downfall. Students will take assessment as seriously as faculty and administrators do. If students are not convinced by the actions of faculty and administrators that assessment is important and that data will be used to improve programs and services, they may not respond to surveys or show up to take tests. Even if they are present, they may not perform conscientiously on such instruments. In Chapter Three, Palomba describes some of these problems and the solutions she and her colleagues have invented at Ball State.

At Truman State, students were among the first to learn of McClain's interest in assessment, because he wrote to them offering them the opportunity to take a nationally standardized test as an additional measure of the extent to which their education was nationally competitive. Later, students served on task forces that helped pilot test new assessment measures and that offered interpretations of the survey responses of students and graduates (Bambenek, 1996).

Insufficient Use of Results. As difficult as it is to convince faculty and students that the collection of assessment data is worthy of their time and effort, arranging the conditions that will encourage them to use the findings may be even harder. The whole constellation of factors associated with success in assessment must be properly aligned to ensure the use of results. Faculty and students must take assessment seriously so that student responses are credible. Instruments must be sufficiently reliable and valid to inspire trust. Findings must be reported as close to the unit level as possible, with comparative data, if usefulness is to be maximized. Administrative and faculty colleagues must establish an atmosphere in which data can be explored fully without fear that weaknesses will be punished. Some resources must be earmarked for improvement efforts so that plans based on assessment findings can actually be implemented rather than put off to a future year.

At Ball State, building assessment into established procedures that are valued by faculty has helped increase the use of assessment findings. In the College of Business, assessment results are reviewed routinely by the curriculum committee. In the College of Sciences and Humanities, any request for program change must be supported with assessment data. As Palomba at Ball State and Hurtgen at Fredonia point out, planning how assessment results will be used as the data collection strategies are devised is one of the best ways to ensure that findings will, in fact, be used.

We know very well that one size does not fit all in assessment. Differences in institutional missions, values, and goals require that assessment approaches be adapted to local conditions on each campus, using what Gray calls "a well-thought-out series of activities that move assessment from innovation to institutionalization" (Chapter One). Nevertheless, we hope that the examples of assessment in practice cited herein, which have endured over periods of ten to twenty-five years, can offer our assessment colleagues some fresh insights into the complex of institutional influences that can either promote or hinder progress in assessment.

References

American Association for Higher Education. *Principles of Good Practice for Assessing Student Learning.* Washington, D.C.: American Association for Higher Education, 1992.

Bambenek, J. J. "Students as Assessors in Institutional Assessment." *Assessment Update,* 1996, 8 (3), 3, 14.

Banta, T. W., and Associates. *Making a Difference: Outcomes of a Decade of Assessment in Higher Education.* San Francisco: Jossey-Bass, 1993.

Banta, T. W., Lund, J. P., Black, K. E., and Oblander, F. W. *Assessment in Practice: Putting Principles to Work on College Campuses.* San Francisco: Jossey-Bass, 1996.

El-Khawas, E. *Campus Trends 1996: Adjusting to New Realities.* Higher Education Panel Report, no. 86. Washington D.C.: American Council on Education, 1996.

Ewell, P. T. "The Current Pattern of State-Level Assessment: Results of a National Inventory." *Assessment Update,* 1996, 8 (3), 1–2, 12–13, 15.

Steele, J. M. "Postsecondary Assessment Needs: Implications for State Policy." *Assessment Update,* 1996, 8 (2), 1–2, 12–13, 15.

TRUDY W. BANTA is vice chancellor for planning and institutional improvement, Indiana University–Purdue University Indianapolis.

INDEX

Academic departments. *See* Discipline-specific assessment; Faculty

Accountability, institutional, 28, 49–50; national emphasis on, 22; for student performance, 18

Accreditation, academic, 75, 77; and assessment evaluation, 32–33, 42, 50–51, 84–85

Administrative leadership, 43–44, 60, 75, 77, 87; and cross-unit communication, 74

Alienation factors, assessment program, 14, 68

Alumni, surveys of, 35, 37, 39, 48–49, 82; statewide information system, 74–75

American Association for Higher Education (AAHE), 80–81

American Association of State Colleges and Universities, 22, 84

American College Test (ACT), 1, 32

Amiran, M. R., 62

Angelo, T. A., 1

Ashcroft, J., 22

Assessment: a common language for, 52, 55; the culture of, 17, 21–22, 26–27, 69; difficulties in drawing conclusions from, 65–66, 67–68; and educational values, 23, 81–82; environmental factors for success of, 21–24, 87–88; externally stimulated, 22, 26, 32; institutionalization of, 8, 22–24, 26–27, 90–91; nonpunitive implementation of, 19–20, 25; ongoing vs. episodic, 24–25, 84–85; ownership issues, 67–68; perceived benefits of, 25–26, 28, 38, 55; perceived disadvantages of, 7, 14–15; planning for response to, 67; and promotion of institutional change, 23–24, 86; and qualitative improvement, 17–18, 23, 25, 33, 45; reporting results of, 39–40, 44; student-centered focus of, 21; uses of results of, 21, 22–24, 27, 37, 43, 49–50, 55, 67, 90

Assessment and accreditation. *See* Accreditation, academic

Assessment goals. *See* Goals

Assessment initiatives: assumptions underlying, 5–6; gradual improvement as

expectation of, 14, 45; timing and persistence of, 22, 24–25

Assessment programs: and accreditation, 84–85; adoption phases and markets, 10–14; areas of strength, 38–41; data distribution strategies, 20, 42, 44, 53; evaluation and improvement of, 14, 50–52, 54, 56; findings and actions, 21–24, 39–40; future challenges for, 27–28, 41–43, 55–57, 67–68; getting started, 17–24, 31–32; initial activities, 20–24, 32–33; involvement of faculty in, 12–15, 23–24, 38–39, 41–42, 51–55, 88–89; involvement of students in, 21, 42–43, 90; multidimensional and sustained, 48–50, 82–83; multidisciplinary, 35–36, 85; obstacles to success of, 26–27, 41–43, 55, 88–91; purposes and uses of, 33, 37, 49–50, 51, 55, 85–86, 90; regional accrediting body evaluation of, 84–85; trust in and support for, 19–20, 88–89; who determines the success of, 6. *See also* specific institution names

Assessment tools and methods: best practices list, 54; limitations of, 89; workbook, 40. *See also* Measurement instruments

At-risk students, 71, 76

Award for Innovation and Excellence, G. Theodore Mitau, 22, 84

Baker, G., 71

Ball State University, 31–45; areas of strength, 38–41; assessment principles and practice at, 82–83, 85, 88, 90

Bambenek, J. J., 90

Banta, T. W., 3, 38, 41, 79, 87

Banta, T. W., and Associates, 1, 79

Benefits of assessment: from external use of results, 49–50; for faculty and pedagogy, 67–68; perceived, 25–26, 28, 38, 55; for specific departments, 54–55

Bennis, W., 8

Black, K. E., 38, 41, 79, 87

Budget resources. *See* Funding for assessment programs

Business administration program, 37

ORDERING INFORMATION

NEW DIRECTIONS FOR HIGHER EDUCATION is a series of paperback books that provides timely information and authoritative advice about major issues and administrative problems confronting every institution. Books in the series are published quarterly in Spring, Summer, Fall, and Winter and are available for purchase by subscription and individually.

SUBSCRIPTIONS cost $54.00 for individuals (a savings of 35 percent over single-copy prices) and $90.00 for institutions, agencies, and libraries. Standing orders are accepted. New York residents, add local tax for subscriptions. (For subscriptions outside the United States, add $7.00 for shipping via surface mail or $25.00 for air mail. Orders *must be prepaid* in U.S. dollars by check drawn on a U.S. bank or charged to VISA, MasterCard, or American Express.)

SINGLE COPIES cost $22.00 plus shipping (see below) when payment accompanies order. California, New Jersey, New York, and Washington, D.C., residents, please include appropriate sales tax. Canadian residents, add GST and any local taxes. Billed orders will be charged shipping and handling. No billed shipments to post office boxes. (Orders from outside the United States *must be prepaid* in U.S. dollars by check drawn on a U.S. bank or charged to VISA, MasterCard, or American Express.)

SHIPPING (SINGLE COPIES ONLY): $30.00 and under, add $5.50; to $50.00, add $6.50; to $75.00, add $7.50; to $100.00, add $9.00; to $150.00, add $10.00.

ALL PRICES are subject to change.

DISCOUNTS FOR QUANTITY ORDERS are available. Please write to the address below for information.

ALL ORDERS must include either the name of an individual or an official purchase order number. Please submit your order as follows:
    Subscriptions: specify series and year subscription is to begin
    Single copies: include individual title code (such as HE82)

MAIL ALL ORDERS TO:
    Jossey-Bass Publishers
    350 Sansome Street
    San Francisco, California 94104-1342

PHONE subscription or single-copy orders toll-free at (888) 378-2537 or at (415) 433-1767 (toll call).

FAX orders toll-free to: (800) 605-2665.

FOR SUBSCRIPTION SALES OUTSIDE OF THE UNITED STATES, contact any international subscription agency or Jossey-Bass directly.

OTHER TITLES AVAILABLE IN THE
NEW DIRECTIONS FOR HIGHER EDUCATION SERIES
Martin Kramer, Editor-in-Chief

UNITED STATES POSTAL SERVICE™

Statement of Ownership, Management, and Circulation
(Required by 39 USC 3685)

1. Publication Title	2. Publication Number	3. Filing Date
NEW DIRECTIONS FOR HIGHER EDUCATION	0 2 7 1 - 0 5 6 0	9/18/97

4. Issue Frequency	5. Number of Issues Published Annually	6. Annual Subscription Price
QUARTERLY	4	$54 - indiv. $90 - instit.

7. Complete Mailing Address of Known Office of Publication *(Not printer) (Street, city, county, state, and ZIP+4)*
350 SANSOME STREET
SAN FRANCISCO, CA 94104
(SAN FRANCISCO COUNTY)

Contact Person
ROGER HUNT
Telephone
415 782 3232

8. Complete Mailing Address of Headquarters or General Business Office of Publisher *(Not printer)*

SAME AS ABOVE

9. Full Names and Complete Mailing Addresses of Publisher, Editor, and Managing Editor *(Do not leave blank)*
Publisher *(Name and complete mailing address)*
JOSSEY-BASS INC., PUBLISHERS
(ABOVE ADDRESS)

Editor *(Name and complete mailing address)*
MARTIN KRAMER
2807 SHASTA ROAD
BERKELEY, CA 94708-2011

Managing Editor *(Name and complete mailing address)*
NONE

10. Owner *(Do not leave blank. If the publication is owned by a corporation, give the name and address of the corporation immediately followed by the names and addresses of all stockholders owning or holding 1 percent or more of the total amount of stock. If not owned by a corporation, give the names and addresses of the individual owners. If owned by a partnership or other unincorporated firm, give its name and address as well as those of each individual owner. If the publication is published by a nonprofit organization, give its name and address.)*

Full Name	Complete Mailing Address
SIMON & SCHUSTER, INC.	P.O. BOX 1172
	ENGLEWOOD CLIFFS, NJ 07632-1172

11. Known Bondholders, Mortgagees, and Other Security Holders Owning or Holding 1 Percent or More of Total Amount of Bonds, Mortgages, or Other Securities. If none, check box ► ☐ None

Full Name	Complete Mailing Address
SAME AS ABOVE	SAME AS ABOVE

12. Tax Status *(For completion by nonprofit organizations authorized to mail at special rates) (Check one)*
The purpose, function, and nonprofit status of this organization and the exempt status for federal income tax purposes:
☐ Has Not Changed During Preceding 12 Months
☐ Has Changed During Preceding 12 Months *(Publisher must submit explanation of change with this statement)*

PS Form **3526**, September 1995 *(See Instructions on Reverse)*

---

13. Publication Title	14. Issue Date for Circulation Data Below
NEW DIRECTIONS FOR HIGHER EDUCATION	SUMMER 1997

15. Extent and Nature of Circulation		Average No. Copies Each Issue During Preceding 12 Months	Actual No. Copies of Single Issue Published Nearest to Filing Date
a. Total Number of Copies *(Net press run)*		1826	1927
b. Paid and/or Requested Circulation	(1) Sales Through Dealers and Carriers, Street Vendors, and Counter Sales *(Not mailed)*	131	72
	(2) Paid or Requested Mail Subscriptions *(Include advertiser's proof copies and exchange copies)*	918	879
c. Total Paid and/or Requested Circulation *(Sum of 15b(1) and 15b(2))* ►		1049	951
d. Free Distribution by Mail *(Samples, complimentary, and other free)*		0	0
e. Free Distribution Outside the Mail *(Carriers or other means)*		223	184
f. Total Free Distribution *(Sum of 15d and 15e)* ►		223	184
g. Total Distribution *(Sum of 15c and 15f)* ►		1272	1135
h. Copies not Distributed	(1) Office Use, Leftovers, Spoiled	554	792
	(2) Returns from News Agents	0	0
i. Total *(Sum of 15g, 15h(1), and 15h(2))* ►		1826	1927
Percent Paid and/or Requested Circulation *(15c / 15g x 100)*		82%	84%

16. Publication of Statement of Ownership
☒ Publication required. Will be printed in the ___WINTER 1997___ issue of this publication.
☐ Publication not required.

17. Signature and Title of Editor, Publisher, Business Manager, or Owner

Susan F. Lewis
SUSAN E. LEWIS
PERIODICALS DIRECTOR
Date 9/18/97

I certify that all information furnished on this form is true and complete. I understand that anyone who furnishes false or misleading information on this form or who omits material or information requested on the form may be subject to criminal sanctions (including fines and imprisonment) and/or civil sanctions (including multiple damages and civil penalties).

Instructions to Publishers

1. Complete and file one copy of this form with your postmaster annually on or before October 1. Keep a copy of the completed form for your records.

2. In cases where the stockholder or security holder is a trustee, include in items 10 and 11 the name of the person or corporation for whom the trustee is acting. Also include the names and addresses of individuals who are stockholders who own or hold 1 percent or more of the total amount of bonds, mortgages, or other securities of the publishing corporation. In item 11, if none, check the box. Use blank sheets if more space is required.

3. Be sure to furnish all circulation information called for in item 15. Free circulation must be shown in items 15d, e, and f.

4. If the publication had second-class authorization as a general or requester publication, this Statement of Ownership, Management, and Circulation must be published; it must be printed in any issue in October or, if the publication is not published during October, the first issue printed after October.

5. In item 16, indicate the date of the issue in which this Statement of Ownership will be published.

6. Item 17 must be signed.

Failure to file or publish a statement of ownership may lead to suspension of second-class authorization.

PS Form **3526**, September 1995 *(Reverse)*